OF CHESHIRE STOCK
THE EARLY HISTORY OF THE
BOSTOCK FAMILY
AND OF THE TIMES IN WHICH THEY LIVED

Tony Bostock

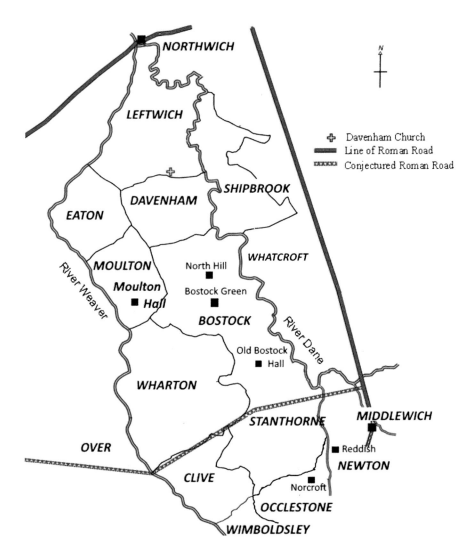

The Home of the Bostocks: the township of Bostock in the very heart of Cheshire and its environs.

Bostock and its Environs (Google Maps)

CONTENTS

PREFACE

Doctor Thomas Fuller, writing in 1612, said that the Cheshire gentry are remarkable for "their numbers, not to be paralleled in England in their like extent of ground; their antiquity; their loyalty; and their hospitality, no county keeping better houses". The men of Cheshire were also described as "a breed of men skilled in the warlike craft - especially archery; accustomed to war; prone to lawlessness; feared and respected throughout the country; and who have a conscious sense of community". The following account of the Bostock family will, I believe, satisfy these descriptions.

In my youth, perhaps when I was about 14 years old, I came across one of a series of articles in a copy of *Cheshire Life* (January 1959) titled – 'Is Your Name.....?' The article in question concerned the name Bostock. It went on to record that the Bostocks were descended from a Saxon named Osmer and that during the medieval period they were lords of the manor of Bostock. The article mentioned a few characters from the past and illustrated the basic shield of arms. Having read this I was both fascinated and instantly addicted to finding out more. For many years thereafter, on Saturday mornings, I journeyed to Manchester Central Library and spent many hours in the local history reference section recording anything I could which was connected to the Bostock name. It was there that I first came across the three gigantic volumes of George Ormerod's *History of the County Palatine and City of Chester* as edited by Thomas Helsby in the late-nineteenth century. Here was what I needed a full account of the family from 1066 through to the sixteenth century. Next, I ventured to the Cheshire Record Office in Chester and began searching the parish registers to find out more, but importantly details of my own family's genealogy. In all I probably spent a good five years of concentrated study which produced much of that which was written down decades later in a detailed type-script booklet *Tailors, Flatmen & Carpenters: The Bostock Family of Northwich & Leftwich (2005)*. This was an account of the medieval history of the name the major branches the village and the hall but being a typed booklet this was only for my immediate family's benefit. Since those days I have occasionally come across additional snippets of information to add to the pile.

In 1978, I produced a small booklet on the basic history of the family name because by that time I was receiving enquiries from other Bostocks who had heard of my research - some from America and Australia. This was then reproduced on the Bostock family web-site *Bostock.net.*

Interest in the family history led me into an interest in the local history of Cheshire generally and particularly the Northwich/Middlewich areas. This recreational pursuit resulted in my reading for a BA in History at Manchester (1991) and an MA in Local History at Keele (1994). Over the years I have published *The Chivalry of Cheshire* (1980); *Owners Occupiers and Others* (2004); *Bostock: a History of a Cheshire Village and its People* (2010); *Winsford: a History of a Cheshire Town and its People* (2016) along with a few other e-books and numerous articles in local history journals, particularly the annual *Cheshire History.*

I recently decided that it was high time that the bulk of my researches into the family be published, not only for my immediate family's benefit, but for the Bostock clan generally, wherever in the world they may be. Hence this work. The popularity of e-books and the relative ease of publication gave me the idea of using this particular format. In order to appeal to a wider audience I have confined this book to the origins and early history of the main family and the major branches.

Another reason for publishing this book is to counter the mis-information about the family and its members that appears on numerous web-sites: many claims are made by various family historians that are without foundation. It is understandable how these mistakes have occurred. The main sources of information are parish registers which go back to the 1530s: any suggestion that a person's baptism or marriage is recorded in a particular parish prior to that time cannot be relied upon. In a passionate desire to link back to the ancient family, genealogist have sought individuals that seem to fit and then latched on to that person. What many do not realise is that the parish registers have many imperfections: register entries were sometimes not made at all or if made pages were lost or damaged. The person one seeks may just not be in the available records. Another problem with the early registers is the sparsity of the record itself - often only the child's name and that of its father are given with no reference to mother or place of residence. The common use of names such as Arthur, George, Thomas and Ralph add to confusion, for example there are so many Arthurs in Cheshire and the rest of England in the mid-sixteenth century that trying to find the correct one without supporting evidence is virtually an impossibility. One has to accept that, at times, the proverbial brick-wall has been encountered, but remain confident and proud that, which ever,

Bostock family it is and wherever in the world the family now live, there is a link back to the original family.

At the end of each chapter, I have made a note of the sources and explained some of the unfamiliar terms used. I must confess that in my youth I failed to make notes of my sources and unfortunately some of them elude me today.

Where quotes from contemporary documents are given the following conventions are used. Abbreviated words have been extended; appropriate capital letters have been employed; dates are given in modern form, and the modern calendar with the beginning of the year as commencing on 1 January has been used; personal and placenames have been modernised and the 'de' form of surnames is dropped. On the subject of personal names, Ralph in its various forms - e.g. Raphe, Ralf, Rannulph - was commonly used by various branches, and throughout this work the name Ralph has been used. The acreages used in the text are invariably Cheshire acres - a Cheshire acre equals about 2.1 modern statute acres. Money is given in the old £. *s. d.* and a mark equalled 13*s* 4*d*.

Finally, words of thanks. After half a decade of research it is difficult to remember who has helped me but if a reader remembers such help then you have my thanks. There is one institution that has certainly helped and that is the Cheshire Record Office (Cheshire Archives and Local Studies), Chester, where there is a superb staff who have been most helpful. The same may be said of the Public Record Office and the British Library in London. For his useful comments and advice over many years I should like to thank Roland Bostock who has done so much research on the spread of the family name and set up the Bostock web-site (www.bostock.net). I also wish to extend my thanks to Martin Goldstraw for his permission to download the marvellous heraldic illustrations from his Cheshire Heraldry web-site (www.cheshireheraldry.org). Finally, a thank you to Mrs Gillian Kent, Clerk of Christ's Church Hospital, Abingdon, for supplying the two Bostock portraits in Chapter 8.

Tony Bostock
Swanlow
Cheshire
January 2017

PREFACE TO SECOND EDITION

It has been five years since I first published *Of Cheshire Stock*. I have decided to republish to amend some typographical mistakes, improve page layouts, add my own heraldic illustrations and to change the cover. Whilst the wording of some paragraphs has been changed, the actual content of the book remains unchanged.

Tony Bostock
Swanlow
Cheshire
May2022

Baptisms 1600 - 1649

Baptisms 1650 - 1699

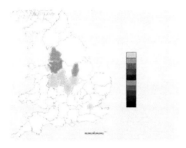

Baptisms 1700 - 1749

Baptisms 1750 - 1799

Baptisms 1800 - 1837

Birth Registrations 1851 - 1860

Birth Registrations 1881 - 1890

Birth Registrations 1951 - 1960

The Spread of the Family Name, c. 1600 - 1960
(Courtesy of Roland Bostock)

1

INTRODUCTION

Sometime ago an audit of the Bostock surname was undertaken using a records of birth to determine the historical spread and density of the surname's occurrence throughout England and Wales. Whilst in the mid-twentieth century the surname occurs in a dozen or more counties with concentrations in the north, as one goes back through the centuries the number of counties in which the name is found reduces significantly until by the beginning of the eighteenth century the name is found in London, the Midlands and the North-West of England with the concentration being in Cheshire. During the 1600s the name was only found in three counties outside London - Nottingham, Shropshire and Cheshire. Research clearly demonstrates that the surname's focus, its home, is the county of Chester. Not only that, the audit also suggests very strongly that the ancestry of anyone with such a name originates in Cheshire and that, in some way, all are connected.

The maps shown opposite are taken from records of christenings and later birth registrations by Roland Bostock. The lighter colour (pink) represents one or less occurrence of the name a year in given periods, whilst the darkest colour indicates between 20 and 25 a year. Before the mid-sixteenth century the name will probably have been limited to Cheshire. The mapping of Roland's audit is certainly good evidence to show that wherever Bostocks now live, their roots are in Cheshire. Anyone in the world - in America, Australia, New Zealand, or elsewhere can also make such a claim. Bostocks are clearly of Cheshire stock.

What then of the origins of the name. English surnames became the fashion in the twelfth century with the purpose of distinguish people with the same given name from one another; gradually these names became hereditary. The etymology of English surnames may be categorised as: 'locative', in that they reflect a general location of residence, such as 'Brook', 'Ford', 'Green', 'Wood', or 'Moor'; or 'habitative' in that they refer to a specific place of residence, such as 'Birmingham', 'Doncaster', 'Preston' or 'London'; 'occupational' in that they refer to a man's trade or business, as with 'Taylor', 'Cook', 'Cooper', 'Smith', 'Wright'; or 'patronymic' suggesting a relationship to someone, such as 'Johnson', 'Peterson', 'Fitzharris' and 'Pritchard' from the Welsh 'ap (son of) Richard'; or else they may be some form of nickname, as with 'Brown', 'Lighfoot', 'King', 'Knight', 'Long', 'Young' and so on. Without doubt the Bostock surname is of the habitative form - it derives from a settlement. Today, in the very heart of Cheshire lies the township of Bostock Green close by the, now lost, ancient settlement of Bostock.

Cheshire, the ancient county of Chester, is situated in north-west England and was formed in the Saxon period, probably in the seventh century, as a distinct area within the Kingdom of Mercia. It is perhaps from about this time that many of the place-names of the county were formed in the new English language, replacing earlier Celtic or British names. So it is with the place-name Bostock.

We have no means of knowing how old the settlement at Bostock is. The fact that the name is Saxon probably takes it back to the seventh or eighth centuries. As to evidence of people in the area prior to that one can only speculate. Immediately to the south ran the Roman road from Chester to Middlewich and a few miles north ran Watling Street, the Roman Road linking Chester with Manchester, whilst the Roman road north out of Middlewich was only a few miles to the east. There have been Roman finds in the neighbouring townships of Moulton and Stanthorne. Remains of a Bronze Age barrow were unearthed in Moulton and at Davenham flint tools have been unearthed. But, it is only with the coming of the Normans in the late-eleventh century that we can definitely put Bostock on the map.

To understand the meaning of the settlement name it is necessary to consider the earliest form of spelling. At the time of the writing of the Domesday Book (1086) the name was spelt *Botestoch*. It is worth noting that the Domesday Book does not refer to what we might today know as 'places' or 'villages', but to manors.[1] The name of the manor is a word formed with two elements - *Bote* and *stoche*. Taking the second element first, this is an Old English, or Saxon, word meaning a secondary settlement or an outlying farm. A place that was subordinate to the more important neighbouring manor of Davenham, which having a *ham* name would suggest a place of higher status and of earlier antiquity. *Stoche* settlements were invariably surrounded by a fence of tree-stumps - hence the word 'stockade'. The first element of the name is derived from a personal name, perhaps an abbreviated form of the Saxon names Bothelm, Botolph, Botsige, or Botwine. It might allude to Saint Botolf, bishop of Thorney, one of the earliest and most revered of East Anglian saints who introduced the Benedictine monastic order into England and became known as the patron saint of wayfarers: he lived in the seventh century. There was also a Saint Botwine, bishop of Ripon, a Northumbrian saint who died in the 780s. Therefore, there are two possible interpretations. Either, a secondary settlement held by a man named 'Bot' (though the female form *Bota* cannot be excluded); or a farm or secondary settlement of Benedictine monks. I prefer the former explanation of the origin of the name.

The name has been spelled in a variety of similar ways - Bostoche, Bostok, Bostocke, and Bostock. During the medieval period many people bearing the surname are recorded with the prefix *de*, i.e. 'of' or 'from' Bostock. In most cases when the name is encountered in medieval documents the *de* refers to a person who was of the family who were the manorial lords of Bostock. It has to be conceded however, that if one of the manorial peasants or tenants moved away he might then be referred to as *de Bostock* in that he/she came from the manor though not necessarily a member of the manorial family. However, in most cases the name will relate to the family. From here on the *de* will not be used.

The site of the Old Bostock Hall and part of the moat

This book will tell the story of the early Bostocks, of how they developed to take their place among the 'middle class' of medieval Cheshire and of some of the characters who emerge during those centuries. Members of the family have been present at some of the major episodes of English history: the thirteenth century Baron's War; the wars against the Scots and the Welsh; the Hundred Years War with France - at the battles of Crecy, Poitiers and Agincourt; the turbulent reign of King Richard II; the Wars of the Roses; in service to Tudor monarchs, and the English Civil War. It will also explore some of the main branches of the family and how they are connected with the main line. Before continuing, it is perhaps worth saying something about medieval society and about Cheshire particularly.

Medieval society was based on the feudal system which structured the society into various categories and followed a set of military and legal protocols. The feudal hierarchy had at its head the king. After him there existed certain classes with decreasing privileges, rights and wealth. This whole structure revolved around the possession of lands and often those lands were given in return for military, administrative and labour services. The king assigned large estates to his tenants-in-chief or barons, which included dukes, earls, bishops and abbots, collectively known as the nobility. Those in this category then farmed out smaller estates and manors to lesser men to obtain required services, especially military service during times of war. These 'lords of the manor' were often knights, holding their lands by 'knights service', but they were not always of such status and might be esquires or gentlemen. Within the manor, the lord of the manor would farm his lands to the ordinary men who would be expected to provide money rents or agricultural labour services for him on his demesne lands, and to follow him to war when the need arose.[2] Those at the bottom of the pile were very often tied to the manor and the will of their lord.

Once established, the middle classes of knights and esquires could improve their lot. The basis of economic prosperity and social status was land and the income derived from it either by direct possession and exploitation, or by leasing. Fortunes could be enhanced by the acquisition of other manors or lands by either purchase or else through carefully negotiated marriage alliances. Incomes could be bolstered by the obtaining of grants from the crown, or in Cheshire's case from the earl. These might be in the form of the wardship, marriage and control of the estates of an under-age heir; a grant of estates that had been declared forfeit for some reason; or the profits of holding an official position in the administration of the county. Lastly there were the profits of war - spoils and ransoms.

During the Middle Ages, Cheshire was one of a few counties which had a unique status. When William the Conqueror was established in England he appointed a number of his vassals to become earls, one of these was the Earl of Chester. For several generations the earldom of Chester was in the hands of a Norman family headed by Hugh d'Avranches, one of the Conqueror's cousins. This independent Norman family became extinct in the early-fourteenth century and the earldom then became an appendage of the Crown for the benefit of the monarch's eldest son. Earl Hugh held his county in its entirety with sovereign rights in order to provide a military frontier against the Welsh and with the intention of eventually subduing his Celtic neighbours. In his turn Hugh, like the king, appointed several tenants-in-chief, his barons, to assist him in defending and ruling the county. Like the king he had a court with a variety of officials and administrators and, in effect, Earl Hugh ruled Cheshire in much the same way as the king ruled England. One of his barons was William Vernon, baron of Shipbrook, whose domain was co-terminus with the parish of Davenham, within which was the manor of Bostock.[3] The lords of the manor of Bostock therefore held their lands by providing service to the Vernon family and their successors.

In telling the story of the Bostock family these aspects of social history and the history of the county will become apparent. This is not just the story of the Bostocks, but of a typical middle-class family of the medieval and the early modern periods of English history.

NOTES AND REFERENCES

1. A 'manor' refers to a unit of land belonging to an individual who was its 'lord'. It an area over which the lord has fiscal and judicial control and could include more than one township: for example the manor of Bostock included Stanthorne and parts of Wharton and Moulton.

2. 'Demesne land' is land retained in a lord's own hands and worked for his benefit, as opposed to land leased to tenants. Under the feudal system land was held from a lord by performance of service, very often military service, *i.e.* 'knight's service', and an estate could be described as being equivalent to so many 'knight's fees'.

3. Earl Hugh created a number of barons to assist him in controlling the county: these were Shipbrook, Kinderton, Halton, Malpas, Dunham, Nantwich (or Malbank), Stockport and Montalt (Mold). Generally, a baron is one who holds a large estate directly from the king or other overlord on the basis of military service.

1.   THE EARLIEST BOSTOCKS: SAXON AND NORMAN TIMES

THE DOMESDAY SURVEY AND THE 'OSMER MYTH'

The family commences with those who adopted the name of the village and manor of Bostock as their surname but, as this style of naming does not occur before the beginning of the thirteenth century, the early history or the family is obscure. A number of theories as to the early genealogy have been put forward, of which the majority quote a descent from a Saxon freeman named Osmer who lived at the time of the Norman conquest. Osmer may have been an important person in the area and perhaps ranked as a 'thane', a man who held directly from the king, or from a nobleman such as the earl of Mercia.

In 1066, Duke William of Normandy conquered England, but it was not until 1070 that Cheshire fell to Norman control. In 1086 a large inventory of the kingdom was made - the Domesday Book. It followed an extensive audit of the kingdom commissioned by King William I, 'the Conqueror'. He required to know how much his kingdom was worth: the extent of the land and resources being owned in England, and the extent of the taxes he could raise. The data gathered records landholders and their tenants, the amount of land they owned, how many people occupied the land (villagers, smallholders, free men, slaves, etc.), the number of ploughs on the land and other resources, the amounts of woodland, meadow, animals, fish. Valuations are given of the land and its assets, before the Norman Conquest, after it, and at the time of the survey. Entries for major towns include records of trade and number of houses. The information collected was recorded in two huge volumes in the space of about a year. However, Domesday is not a complete gazetteer of eleventh century England - many places are not recorded - neither is it an accurate assessment of population. So far as Cheshire is concerned the manorial entries are briefer than those in other counties.

According to the Domesday Book, Osmer was the Saxon lord of Bostock and nine other manors during the reign of Edward the Confessor (1042-1066); whether he was still alive in 1086 is not clear. Some references to him on internet sites originating in America call him 'Osmer de Bostock' at a time when surnames were rare and certainly not the norm, and others, quite incorrectly call him 'Oliver de Bostock' - further he may never have lived in Bostock. Some web-sites say he was born in Normandy; that he was born in

1026 or 1029; that he was son of a 'Hugh fitzRichard', another Norman; had a son named Hugh who was born in Normandy in 1055, and that both father and son died at the Battle of Hastings - all pure fiction. For example how can anyone state a place and date of birth from this time is ridiculous. It is extremely unlikely that a Norman would use a Saxon name or that a Norman was the holder of Cheshire estates under Edward the Confessor. Likewise, as there are no lists of people serving at Hastings, the circumstances of his death can be dismissed as being without proof.

The Domesday Book entry - the first written reference to the name.
(Ref: www.opendomeday.org/place/SJ6769/bostock/)

The name of the alleged Bostock progenitor is a rare one. The name occurs in a number of manors outside Cheshire. In Derbyshire 'Osmer the priest' held property in Derby; in Dorset an 'Osmar' held the manors of Bowood, Buckham, and Wellwood; and there are a few references in the West Country. In Cheshire a man named Osmer held the manors of Shipbrook, Davenham, Bostock, Audlem, Crewe and Claverton (near Chester). He was also held a share in the manors of Leftwich, Austerston, Wistaston and Frith (a lost settlement in Wrenbury parish). It can be claimed with reasonable certainty that the same man is referred to in each instance. Whilst these properties were somewhat dispersed there was a clear focus on the ancient parish of Davenham. In all Osmer's lands contained about twenty-four ploughlands (about 1500 Cheshire acres, or 3100 statute acres), large tracts of woodland, with a number of enclosures and nesting places for hawks, and meadows. In the time of King Edward the value of these lands was a little over £6 but by 1086 they were worth about £2 less. For taxation purposes his lands were assessed as being about ten hides. His richest holding was Claverton, a few miles south of Chester, which was valued at £2, both before and after the Conquest. Here the available arable land was estimated as being two ploughlands. To this manor belonged eight burgess properties in the city of Chester, another two on the other side of the River Dee in Handbridge, and a salthouse in Northwich.

Agriculturally, and perhaps territorially, the largest manors were those of Shipbrook and Audlem each of which had enough land for five ploughs and were worth twenty shillings in 1066. By comparison, Bostock was small having only two ploughlands (about 125 Cheshire acres or about 262 statute acres) and worth only three shillings.

It is said that much of Cheshire was wasted and depopulated during the punitive expedition made by the Conqueror in 1070: Osmer's manors may have suffered accordingly. The phrase *waste inven* ('found to be waste') recorded by the Domesday scribes is perhaps testimony to the Norman destruction of the shire, but it may simply mean the manor was of no value to its lord. Osmer was dispossessed in favour of Norman warriors. Hugh d'Avranches, the newly appointed Earl of Chester who had been granted the whole of the county by William the Conqueror, granted Shipbrook, Leftwich, Davenham, Bostock, Audlem and Crewe to Richard le Vernon as part of his barony of Shipbrook. The manors of Austerston, Wistaston and Frith were granted to William Malbedeng, baron of Wich Malbank (Nantwich), and Claverton was granted to Hugh fitz Osbern, another of earl Hugh's barons.

Between the years 1070 and 1086 there was some recovery in the values of the places found to be waste so that, by the time of the Survey, most places had recovered fifty per cent of their pre-Conquest valuation. However, whilst both Shipbrook and Audlem had lands that were not being worked to the full capacity of their five ploughlands, and had valuations which dropped by fifty per cent, the value of the lands at Bostock increased three-fold. Along with Claverton, Bostock was worked to its full capacity of two ploughlands (about 120 Cheshire acres). The prosperity of this manor may have something to do with the fact that the baron of Shipbrook held no demesne land here and that the three radmen and their two serfs who are recorded as living on the manor worked the arable lands for themselves. Radmen, who account for only eight per cent of the recorded population in Cheshire, seem to have been freemen who did some form of riding services for their lord in return for which they received a share in the fields: such men might be either Norman or Saxon. The serfs were the unfree labourers who were tied to the manor and their lord - in all probability subservient to the radmen.

It may be that Osmer, the alleged progenitor of the Bostock family, never actually resided at Bostock, as before the Conquest it was his poorest manor. It is more likely that he resided either at Shipbrook or Audlem. Likewise, after the Conquest it is unlikely that he lived at Bostock, though a relative might have done so. From the late-eleventh century the manor of Bostock became the home of a family who where tenants of the Vernon family, the barons of Shipbrook, but exactly who they were during the eleventh and twelfth centuries is a matter of conjecture - but, whomever they were, over time they became known by the name of their residence.

In conclusion, it is reasonable to say that the Bostock family might have been descendants of Osmer the Saxon. But, equally, they might stem from one of the three radmen, one of whom could conceivably have been Osmer's son or in some way related to him. The family may even be Norman in origin, perhaps a junior branch of the Vernon family who assumed the name of their place of residence as other branches of that family, and others, often did.

The Domesday Manors held by Osmer.
The underlined names are those of the Hundreds (administrative districts) of Cheshire.

THEORIES OF EARLY DESCENT

Various antiquaries and historians of the Tudor period believe that Osmer was the 'original' Bostock and produced descents from him. However, as already said, any link back to Osmer has to be taken with some scepticism as it was 'fashionable' in Elizabethan times to try to prove Saxon ancestry as a result many claims were made without a shred of proof. The heralds of the College of Arms in their *Visitation of Cheshire 1580*, recorded that Adam de Bostock, who was living circa 1300, was the son of Sir Edward, son of Sir William (and Elizabeth Audley), son of Henry, son of Sir Warren (and Havice de Quincy), son of Ranulf (and Margaret Vernon), son of Gilbert, who would have been born about 1130. He was son of Roger, son of Richard, son of Hugh, son of Osmer the Saxon, which would mean that Osmer was born about 1030. An illuminated pedigree made about 1580 by William Smith, a herald who bore the title Rouge Dragon Pursuivant of Arms, certainly records this particular lineage.[1]

The seventeenth-century antiquary, Piers Leycester of Tabley, suggests that Adam de Bostock was the son of Sir Edward (and a daughter of the Trumpington family), son of William (and Elizabeth), son of Arthur (and Bridget Blundeville), son of Henry (and Eleanor Poole), son of Warren (and Havice), son of William (and Margaret Vernon), son of Gilbert, son of Roger, son of Richard, son of Osmer, son of 'Hugh fitz Richard, lord of Bostock under Edward the Confessor'. The genealogist John Booth, writing in the mid-seventeenth century, gives a similar descent. However, as mentioned above, 'Osmer son of Hugh fitz Richard' is too improbable to accept as Osmer is a Saxon name and Hugh fitz Richard sounds Norman, but if correct it would push the family history back two generations before the Conquest and would give the family something of a unique status.

Although there are minor variations as to their order, the suggested pedigrees give nine generations between Adam and Osmer, and this, on the basis of 23 years between generations, means that Osmer was born in the early to mid-eleventh century and was a middle-aged man at the time of the battle of Hastings. More realistically, the pedigree of the Bostock family of Sittingbourne, Kent, as recorded in Burke's *Landed Gentry*, and accepted by the College of Arms, records the ancient pedigree only so far back as Randolph son of Gilbert.

George Ormerod, the celebrated nineteenth century Cheshire historian, in the third volume of his enormous *History of the Palatine of Chester*, agrees with Edward Williamson, another seventeenth century antiquarian, and says: "Dr. Williamson, who very properly doubts the descent from Osmer, says, that 'we may be assured by Inquisition 2 Hen. II, yt Warine de Bostock (second husband of Havice, daughter to Hugh Gyffylliog, 5th earl of Chester), was ye son of Randle, son of Adam Bostock'." Ormerod then says that Warren was the father of Gilbert, who was father of William, father of Philip, father of Adam. I have so far been unable to trace the inquisition of 1156, which was probably an *inquisition post mortem*[2]. There is no evidence that Williamson is correct.

There are certainly a number of common factors in the pedigrees quoted. Each mentions a Gilbert, son of Roger (I would compute that Gilbert was born circa 1130) and these two may occur in a document of 1174 which relates to the marriage of Amice, one of the daughters of Earl Hugh of Chester to Randle Mainwaring of Warmingham and Peover. With his daughter the earl gave to Randle 'the services of Gilbert son of Roger' which amounted to the service of one knight. Whilst there is nothing in the deed to further identify Gilbert or his father it is interesting to note that when, in 1455, the main line of the Mainwaring family died out, and the succession of the lords of the manor became uncertain, a John Bostock was presented to the people of Warmingham as the lord's esquire and deputy: it was said that he was descended of the Gilbert son of Roger. There may be some truth in this given that a junior line of the Bostocks of Bostock lived at Elton in Warmingham parish for many centuries, and the main line of the family held lands in neighbouring Occlestone and Wimboldsley.

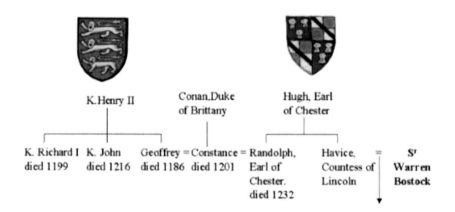

Royal Connections from Warren's alleged marriage to Havice

Another common factor is the marriage of Warren de Bostock and Havice, a daughter of Earl Hugh Gyffylliog (1155-1181). The earl was born in 1147 and married Beatrix, daughter of Lord Lucy, justiciar of England, by whom he had Randolph, who became the 6th earl, and six daughters. One of these daughters was Havice, born circa 1180, who married Roger, earl of Lincoln, and when he died in 1217, the earldom was transferred to her brother. On

Randolph's death in 1252 the earldom of Lincoln passed back to Havice who then became countess of Lincoln. From her the title passed to John de Lacy, baron of Halton, husband of her daughter Margaret. If Warren did marry this daughter of the earl of Chester then it was a most important match and subject no doubt of much criticism at the time, however the alleged marriage is without any documentary proof. Havice would have had children of her first marriage in the early 1200s, and by any second husband in the 1220s. These dates would certainly fit with both pedigrees which would have Warren being born circa 1185: a little younger than Havice. Satisfied with the evidence, the College of Arms allowed the Bostock family to incorporate the arms of the earldoms of Chester and Lincoln into their armorial achievement. This alleged link with the family of the Norman earls of Chester is interesting, because, if true, it means that Warren was related to the Kings of England of the time!

Whilst on the subject of early versions of descent there a curious and spurious claim made by the Tudor antiquary and historian Laurence Bostock, the author of many manuscripts on the family and on Cheshire generally written in the 1570s. In one of his note books he took the family back to the mid-fifth century! Robert Cook, Clarenceux King of Arms, wrote a copy of Laurence's alleged descent.[3] The passage (with text modernised) reads as follows:

> *"Barbew, inhabiting about the river of Albis in Saxonia, came into Great Britain, with a great number of Saxons in the company of the Duke of Angria in 449. Which Saxons conquered the said Britons and drove them into the mountains, now called Wales, where they remain to this day. The said Barbew for his worthy service had given him (in part of recompense) the lordship of Botestok, now called Bostok, lying in the county if Chester, near to the forest of Delamere, in the parish of Davenham: and he had issue as followeth: ......".*

A family tree is then drawn starting with Frances de Bostok who had two sons – Conrad and Baldwin. The descent then continues down from Conrad with Albert, Friderik and Ludowik. This last person is given a marriage to the 'daughter and heir of Lucas, earl of Chester, before the Conquest'. The descent continues with Philip; Geoffrey; Charles, who married a daughter of 'Borcell'; Sir Raffe who married Eleanor the heiress of John Poole; Sir Arthur who married an heiress of Holford; and Sir Warren who married Havice of Chester. Laurence continues with what is similar to the descents mentioned above: Sir Henry, Sir William who married an Audley; Sir Edward who married a Ferrers; Sir Adam who married a Winnington; Sir William; and Sir Adam who married a Wetenhall. Cook also adds notes made by a 'D. Powell' which alleges a number of marriages to the earliest generations: *i.e.* that Baldwin married Angarad, daughter of Cadell, Prince of South Wales; that Conrad married Wenefrid daughter of Cradok, King of Hawarden; Frences married Beatrice daughter to the Duke of Britaine (presumably Brittany); Albert married Elenor daughter of the Duke of Anguis (perhaps Angus); and Friderik married Agnes daughter if Kynan Prince of North Wales. To say the least Laurence's pedigree is fanciful and what is particularly noticeable is that there is no mention of Osmer! Enough said.

EARLY USE OF THE NAME

It is impossible to determine the exact nature of the descent of the main line of the family – those who were lords of the manor of Bostock. All that can be done is to mention various individuals as they occur. The first use of the surname occurs in what seems to be a late-twelfth century document: although the deed is without date its approximate period can be estimated by reference to the witnesses who are all members of the Vernon family. The charter is a surrender of fishing rights in the River Dane by Gilbert Bostock in favour of his lord, the baron of Shipbook, which is quoted at the head of the pedigree drawn up in the *Visitation of Cheshire*[4] Underneath is a drawing of a seal showing an eagle which is supposed to be that of Sir Gilbert Bostock. A drawing of the Bostock arms is then shown beneath the words 'William son of Gilbert Bostock surrenders to Warin Vernon'.

A deed of about 1190, by which lands in Tabley were given to Adam de Dutton, lists witnesses among whom is the name 'Gilb. B'to', an abbreviated form of Gilbert Bostock. Another early document is dated 1218 which mentions Gilbert and a son William Bostock among witnesses to the grant of the manor of Marbury made by Warren Vernon to his son William (later surnamed 'de Merebury').[5] Another Gilbert appears in documents about this time. On 30 November 1233, a Gilbert Bostock was the plaintiff in a case, which was later dropped and he was amerced 12*d* for his trouble. A Gilbert Bostock occurs in 1288 as the plaintiff in a case before the County Court involving Randle Praers involving possession of land in Landican on the Wirral: Gilbert withdrew from the action and was fined 12*d*.[6] A Gilbert also occurs as late as 1297.[7]

William, son of Gilbert Bostock, is a much more identifiable character for he occurs in a number of documents of the mid-thirteenth century. At some time during the early years of King Henry III (1216-1272) and when Philip d'Orreby was justiciar of Chester (1209-1229), William, grandson of Warren Bostock, acknowledged in the County Court, that he held his lands from Warren Vernon, baron of Shipbrook, by ploughing and shearing his lord's demense lands.[8] It is likely that William, probably aged about twenty-one, was appearing in the court to prove his age and establish his right to inherit his father's lands and, if this was towards the end of Orreby's term of office, i.e. between 1216 and 1229, William was born circa 1200.

Between 1255 and 1295, a William Bostock frequently occurs in documents relating to the town of Middlewich and its salt industry. In the later year he is styled 'lord of Bostock' but if it is the same man he will have been a great age. On one occasion he is styled as 'son of Gilbert'. From these deeds it seems that the Bostocks held properties in the borough of Middlewich. Members of the Croxton family were mentioned in some of the deeds and it seems that they were related to the Bostocks: at some time during the reign of Henry III (1216-1272) a John Croxton married Amice, daughter of William Bostock.[9]

In 1259 and 1260, a William Bostock appeared before the County Court charged with certain offences contrary to the strict forest laws. At this period of time there was much controversy as to the way in which men who contravened the laws should be dealt with and as to who should preside over the courts and sit in judgement. The passages relating to William mention the arguments that were made. In 1249, the Lord Edward, Prince of Wales and Earl of Chester, appointed an escheator into the pattern of government of the county, who was also to serve as warden of the forests and preside over the courts that heard forest offences.[10] The people of Cheshire complained that such an official was novel and contrary to custom and that it should be the justiciar of the county who should hear such cases.[11] When William's case was being heard a letter from the Prince was read to all the barons, knights and freemen attending the court ordering them to obey Sir Thomas d'Orreby, his escheator and warden of the forests. They refused to do so. Sir Thomas ordered that William Bostock's property be seized by the sheriff as security for his eventual appearance at the court at a later date for trial, he having made a complete denial of the charges. The community, hearing of this decision objected, saying that only the justiciar could 'attach' men to the court and take sureties. Nevertheless, William probably did appear in court some time later and was probably bound over to keep the forest laws. The outcome of the dispute was that the Lord Edward, in September 1260, allowed forest offences to be heard by the justiciar sitting in the County Court. In June of that year,

William, with his daughter Amice and a Philip Bostock, occurs in the court regarding a matter of dower.[12]

Another William occurs in the 1280s. In 1280, a William Bostock was a juror in a case heard to determine the extent of the manor of Frodsham upon the discovery of the treason of David, lord of Frodsham, the brother of Llewellyn, Prince of Wales. In the same year, William appears as a juror at an *inquisition post mortem*. In 1288, William served on the jury of the County Court and then on 22 February 1289, he was the plaintiff in a case against Nicholas Hova concerning a piece of woodland in Moulton, a township that lies just west of Bostock: William lost the action and was fined 40*d*.[13] At the same time he claimed possession of another piece of woodland in the same township, this time against a cousin, Philip Bostock, but Philip defended the action by saying he was only claiming a pigsty in the wood, which his father had held as part of his free tenement in Bostock.[14] This Philip probably held lands in Bostock and nearby Moulton. He had a grandson named Adam, who in 1354 claimed to hold, along with a number of other persons, lands in Bostock, Moulton and Davenham from 'Adam, son of Adam Bostock', his kinfolk and the senior line of the family. A little while later the case involving Hova arose again when William claimed that the original jury was false sworn and that the case was wrongly decided against him. Hova insisted that in the time of his father Randle he was possessed of the entire wood, to do with as he pleased, assarting, taking pannage, taking honey, etc.[15] A new jury of twenty-four local people agreed with him and again found against William who was then sent to the local gaol for making a false claim: he later paid a fine and was released. It is possible that this William was a Bostock 'of Moulton' and not 'of Bostock'.

William Bostock may have had a brother named Hugh who appears in the County Court in 1260.[16] Hugh and William occur together as witnesses to a number of local deeds especially various grants made by members of the neighbouring Clive family in the mid-thirteenth century. In documents relating to the administration of Middlewich, Hugh is sometimes referred to as the bailiff of the town. Hugh also appears as a witness to a number of other deeds without William: about 1234, he witnessed a grant made by Gralam Lostock to Richard Grosvenor, and a deed made by a member of the Clive family in favour of the same Richard Grosvenor. About the year 1272, both William and Hugh witnessed a grant made by Robert Croxton to the Abbey of St. Werburgh.[17] The most interesting document to mention Hugh can be dated 1269/70. It states that Alice, the widow of Richard Helsby, gave to Hugh an annual rent of two shillings issuing from property in Bridge Street, Chester, and that the grant was to continue to Hugh's heirs born to him by Alice's daughter, Havice. The deed is witnessed by Alice's brother, Peter Thornton, and by 'Joceram brother of lord Philip, brother of William de Bostock'. This tells us not only who Hugh married but also mentions two of William's brothers. Philip occurs mainly during the period 1259-1288 and on one occasion appears in a suit for dower dated 1259/60 which also mentions Amice, daughter of William Bostock. Philip also appears in Middlewich charters and in some of them he is styled 'dominus' (lord), which may not mean, as some have considered, that he was lord of Bostock for it may be a courtesy title as often used to describe clerics. In fact, a 'Philipo clerico' occurs in the mid-thirteenth century and he might be the same person.

Another Bostock about this time was Roger. In August 1260, he appeared before the County Court to defend himself against John Barker of Middlewich and his wife Ellen, and Richard Golde and his wife, who were claiming three 'oxgangs' of land in Moulton as their inheritance. Roger claimed he had lawful possession and had a charter which had been burnt in a house fire. The jury were satisfied as to the fire and therefore found in his favour.[18]

A CONFUSING TIME

As said before it is impossible to be sure of the genealogy in these early years. It seems that there were two Williams, one as the lord of Bostock and the other living at Moulton, or else the two men represent two generations of a William Bostock with the first being born circa 1200 and the other circa 1235. The first seems to have had sons William, Philip, James, Hugh and Gilbert. The second William may then have been the son and heir and if so this would account for the name occurring between 1213 and 1272, it is either that or William lived a very long time! There may also have been two generations with a Hugh Bostock: the Hugh who acted as a witness in 1234 must then have been of age and therefore born circa 1210 or earlier, whereas it is likely that the grant of 1269/70 was shortly after the marriage between Hugh and Havice. William's last son, Gilbert resided in Tarporley and heads the descent of the Bostocks of that township. He had a son William who married Margaret, daughter of Thomas Vernon of Lostock, and a grandson, John, who was a chaplain at Chester Cathedral in 1330. From Gilbert descended a branch who resided at Maceray End, Wheathampstead, Hertfordshire. On the floor of the north transept in the church of St Helen, is a brass to Hugh Bostock and Margaret (née Maceray) with indentations for three sons and three daughters: there are four shields but only one remains bearing three bats. In 1420, Hugh's son, John Bostock, often surnamed 'de Whethamstead', became abbot of St. Albans and a well-known person of his day due to his friendship with Humphrey, Duke of Gloucester, and for his writings about the Wars of the Roses (see Chapter 8).

According to the pedigree in Burke's *Landed Gentry*, a William Bostock fought at the battle of Evesham in October 1265. The Battle of Evesham was one of the two main battles of thirteenth century 'Second Barons' War': the first had been the Battle of Lewes a year earlier following which Simon de Montfort, Earl of Leicester, and the rebellious barons, gained control of Parliament. Evesham marked the defeat of the Montfort party inflicted by Lord Edward, earl of Chester and later King Edward I, who led the forces of his father, King Henry III. If correct William Bostock was probably aged about thirty, and may also have been at the siege of Beeston Castle (1264) in an effort to rid it of Montfort's followers. One of the commanders at the siege was Hugh Audley, lord of Stratton Audley, Oxfordshire, who had a daughter, Elizabeth, who is said to have married a William Bostock. Others say that William Bostock's father-in-law was James Audley, lord of Audley and Heleigh, Staffordshire. William may have married a second time for, in 1305, a lady named Amice, described as his widow, sued John Arclid for dower. Whilst on the subject of military matters English armies regularly fought against the Welsh Princes in North and South Wales and on these occasions many Cheshire men were expected to serve in the earl of Chester's retinue on these campaigns. In the early 1270s, a force of 1,000 Cheshire men, comprising archers and foot soldiers, formed part of an army of 2,576 raised by the sovereign for service in Wales. In 1277, about 620 men from Cheshire went into North Wales as reinforcements. In January 1283, an army 5,000 strong served in Wales of whom 2,000 were Cheshire men. Normally the men of Cheshire could not be compelled to serve in South Wales but in 1287 a special request was made and consequently several hundred assisted in quelling a rebellion there. In the Welsh rebellions of 1295 the county had 1,300 men serving in North Wales.

On the subject of the Audley marriage Laurence Bostock wrote in his note book that in 1201, William Bostock married a daughter of Lord Audley but doesn't give first names. He also says that the couple had three sons: Edward, Richard and Raffe, the last of whom was given the manor of Moulton by his father.[19] He then copies the deed by which the manor was granted. In brief, it says that Raffe was to have all the lands formerly held by Warren Vernon, 2½ acres formerly held by Henry Cademan and a piece of waste land alongside the River Weaver, in return for the payment of two shillings a year. The witnesses include a Philip Bostock. The same manuscript also notes that a William Moulton, who was lord of the manor of Moulton during the reign of King William II (Rufus) had an only daughter who married the lord of Bostock and thus conveyed Moulton to the Bostock family. This is the first instance of the Bostocks obtaining additional property by marriage.

Most pedigrees state that William and Elizabeth had a son named Edward, but apart from Laurence's notes there is no documentary evidence of a man of this name in the thirteenth century. Piers Leycester states that Edward married a daughter of the Trumpington family; an interesting suggestion as between 1330-1363 a Roger Trumpington held the advowson of Davenham church through a marriage to one of the heiresses to the barony of Shipbrook - but this is much too late. This Roger would be the son of the knight of the same name who is immortalised by the famous brass to his memory in Trumpington church, Cambridgeshire. Ormerod states that one of the Vernon heiresses, Auda, married a William Stafford, 'alias Trumpwyn'.

Before leaving this section on the early Bostock family some mention must be made of other marriages that are alleged for these times. A marriage for which there is no real evidence is that between a Ralph Bostock and Margaret, daughter and heiress of Warren Vernon, baron of Shipbrook: Leycester says that she was the widow of Richard Wilbraham. In the Bostock pedigree such a marriage would have taken place during the middle years of the twelfth century - about one hundred years before the heiresses of Vernon divided up the barony amongst their husbands, one of whom was indeed a Richard Wilbraham. Despite this, the Heralds allowed the arms of the Vernon family alluding to this alleged marriage to be incorporated in the Bostock coat of arms. Ranulph and Margaret are supposed to have had a son named Henry, though there is no documentary evidence for him. The early pedigrees show Henry married to Eleanor, daughter and heiress of Robert Poole of Poole. Though he died leaving a number of daughters the Poole pedigrees do not show any daughter as marrying a Henry Bostock and the arms of the Poole family are not included in the Bostock achievement of arms allowed in 1580.

In this next period the evidence of the descent of the family is on somewhat firmer ground, though to begin with it is still a little shaky.

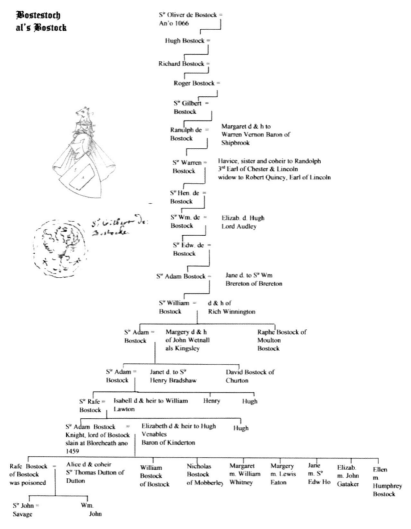

The Bostocks of Bostock as shown in the Visitation of Cheshire 1580
(The illustrations appear in the original among the Harleian Manuscripts.)

The majority of the information provided comes from Ormerod's History of Cheshire, vol. iii. I have referred to Piers Leycester's pedigree - this was recorded in a fine volume of pedigrees of Cheshire families written by him in the seventeenth century. Many years ago I had sight of this work but since then all trace of it alludes me. Reference has been made to information published in Burke's *Landed Gentry* where a genealogy of the Bostock family of Sittingbourne, Kent, is detailed: the reliability of the early generations in that source cannot be guaranteed. Mention has also been made of the herald's *Visitation of Cheshire, 1580*, as published by the Harleian Society: the original is with the British Library. Recently papers in the Harleian manuscript collection at the British Library have been consulted, especially the papers of Laurence Bostock in Harl. MS. 139, 245, 2059, and Harl MS. 1500 f.24. Harl. 1500 f. 24 is a large pedigree compiled by William Smith, Rouge Dragon Pursuivant of Arms about 1580. Smith was from the family settled in Warmingham and his mother was Jane Bostock, daughter of Ralph Bostock.

In the Domesday section there is reference to a 'hide'. This was a unit of taxation based on both the measure of land and its associated resources on a manor. Whilst some historians have placed an acreage to the hide, it would vary from place to place depending on the quality of soil and would be variable depending on other resources.

1.'Visitations' were periodic inspections of the counties made by the Heralds from London who then recorded, confirmed or approved the coats of arms and pedigrees of the gentry. For Cheshire the Visitations of 1580 and 1613 have been published. British Library, Harl. Mss.1500, f.24 and Harl.2094,f.42.
2. An enquiry into the value and extent of a deceased person's estate. It was also responsible for establishing who was the rightful heir.
3. Harl.245, f.166.
4. Ormerod, G., *History of the County Palatine of Chester*, edited by T. Helsby, 2nd ed. (1882). vol. I, p.471
5. *Ibid*, p. 633.
6. Tait, J., (ed.), 'The Chartulary or Register of the Abbey of St. Werburgh, Chester', part II, *Chetham Society*, vol. 82, (1923), p.404. 'Dower' is that part of a man's estate, normally a third, which the widow enjoys during her life. It can also be that property which she brought to her husband in marriage.
7. Harl.245, f.162v

8. Ormerod, from whom this passage is quoted, suggests that this is a relic of villein tenure that seems to give some colour to the statement of the descent from the Saxon Osmer. In reality it does not, though it may indicate descent from one of the three radmen of Domesday as mentioned above. In any event the suggestion that William was of villein status is probably incorrect as he seems to be on a higher status.

9. The documents relating to the town were compiled by William Vernon in the 17th century and published in two volumes by the Chetham Society in 1941 and 1944, see Varley, Joan, (ed.), *A Middlewich Chartulary*.

10. Stewart-Brown, op cit, pp.2,14. Forests were designated tracts for ground, which included arable areas, scrubland, woodland, heath and moor, for the purpose of hunting. Severe penalties were inflicted upon anyone who broke the laws of the forest which were designed to preserve the natural habitat. The word 'forest comes from the Latin *forinsec* meaning outside and therefore an area outside the normal customary law of England.

11. An 'escheator' was an official of the royal court who was responsible for seizing into the king's hands freehold land for which there was no legitimate heir, or when the heir was under age.

12. 'Justiciar' - a judge, often the chief justice for the county.

13. Stewart-Brown, *op cit*, p.22

14. *Ibid*, p.95

15. *Ibid*, pp.128,129

16. *Ibid*, p.132.

17. 'Assarting' clearing woodland or waste land for cultivation; 'pannage' is the right to feed pigs in the lord's woodlands.

18. Stewart-Brown, *op cit*, p.18.

19. Harl.245, f.164

THE FOURTEENTH CENTURY

ADAM I BOSTOCK (C.1275 - C.1350)

Adam Bostock, son of Edward, if we are to believe the ancient pedigrees, or Philip, if Ormerod is correct, which is to be doubted, but more likely son of William, was born about 1275 and seems to be the first of many to bear this first name. An 'Adam son of William Bostock' appears in the rolls of the County Court for the years 1303/4 which adds an extra degree of confusion.

It is said that Adam was knighted at the battle of Falkirk, 22 July 1298, during Edward I's Scottish campaign and was actually knighted by the king at the event.[1] I have found no proof of what is stated in Burke's *Landed Gentry*, though it is known that about 1,000 men were requisitioned from Cheshire for service on the campaign so it is highly likely, but to suggest he was knighted at the battle is perhaps something of an exaggeration. In 1310, he acted as one of the king's purveyors for the Northwich Hundred in preparation for an expedition to Scotland. Adam added to the family's property in 1321/2, by obtaining lands in neighbouring Wharton, then known as 'Waverton juxta Bostok'.

In the first half of the fourteenth century Adam witnessed several Middlewich charters and seems to have taken the place of the William Bostock who witnessed so many in the last half of the previous century: this would certainly suggest he had become the new lord of Bostock. In 1323, Adam occurs as a witness to a deed relating to the Davenport family, and in the next year he occurs with John Ward, Randol Merton and others as sureties for a Richard Waryhull. Seven years later, Adam and others, including Hugh Venables, baron of Kinderton, entered into a recognizance of £52, to the king for the bailiwick of Northwich, which they took to farm for two years.[2] On 17 March 1333, he and eight other persons took the profits of the 'advowries' of the county.[3] An inquiry held in 1334 found that it was not to the earl's damage for Adam to close a highway, some forty feet wide and forty perches long, leading from *Balshagh*, through Bostock, to Middlewich, on the understanding that Adam created another way in lieu of it. (*Balshagh* was probably located somewhere in Davenham).

In the next year Adam appears again. This time he seems to have been involved in a number of local feuds for he and a neighbour, Richard Croxton, were bound over to keep the peace towards a member of the Warburton family;

similarly, in 1342 he and William Brereton were bound to keep the peace towards John Wrenbury. Such disputes probably arose over arguments concerning rights to lands or the boundaries between them.

On 3 May 1343, we find Adam Bostock styled the elder in a grant to Nicholas, son of Richard Vernon of Whatcroft, of a parcel of lands in Bostock that lay between Whatcroft Hall and the River Dane, on the occasion of Nicholas' marriage to Adam's daughter, Margery. The witnesses included Sir Hugh Venables and Sir Hugh Vernon. A few years later an indenture was made out that recited the settlement of a dispute concerning *hopurfre* and *tollfre* at Bostock mill between Nicholas Vernon's son Ralph and Adam, 'lord of Bostocke'.[4] It was agreed at a hearing held in Davenham that Adam had granted Ralph free multure forever on the understanding that whenever he visited the mill Ralph would grind whatever corn was already in the hopper, regardless of who owned it, before grinding his own. Further it was agreed that if both Adam and Ralph delivered their grain at the same time then each was to grind a quarter of their load at a time. The witnesses to this agreement included Sir Ralph Vernon, Sir Hugh Dutton, Sir Roger Chedle and Sir William Brereton.

Adam died at sometime shortly before 1350 when his widow Matilda occurs in suit for dower against John de St. Pierre of four messuages and sixty acres of land in Bostock.[5] The St. Pierre family had obtained over-lordship of the manor of Bostock by marriage during the break-up of the barony of Shipbrook amongst a number of daughters of Sir Warren Vernon who died without a male heir. Whilst the manor of Bostock was held by service initially from the Vernons and then from the St. Pierres, the Bostocks also held other lands in the area directly from the earl of Chester.

The ancient pedigrees state that this Adam married Jane, daughter of Sir William Brereton of Brereton. However, according to the Brereton pedigree and her likely time of birth, this marriage is more likely to be that of Adam's son of the same name. Adam seems to have had the following children: Adam II, William, Ralph, David and Margery.

ADAM II AND WILLIAM BOSTOCK

The next lord of the manor of Bostock is usually given as William de Bostock, but this is to be doubted as a document of 1343 refers to 'Adam de Bostok, senior' and a document which appears in the *Black Prince's Register* indicates that in the 1350s an 'Adam son of Adam de Bostok' was the lord of the manor.[6] In 1354, Hamon Bret of Davenham, 'Adam son of Adam son of Philip de Bostok', Hugh Ward of Bostock, William Moulton, Richard Bret of Moulton, and William son of Robert Davenham, jointly made a complaint to Edward, Prince of Wales (commonly known today as 'the Black Prince'), in his capacity as earl of Chester. It seems that they had been ordered to pay 6*d* an acre to the Prince for their lands and tenements in Bostock, Davenham and Moulton in the belief that they held directly from him as earl. They argued that this was not so and that they held their lands from 'Adam son of Adam de Bostok', who held the manor of Bostock from John de St. Pierre. An order, dated 21 February 1355, required the matter to be investigated on the Prince's behalf, and a further order was made on 11 May requiring further evidence to be heard. Therefore, it seems clear, firstly, that William Bostock was not the lord of Bostock at this time and, secondly, that the line of 'Adam son of Adam son of Philip' was a parallel, yet junior, line of Bostocks (they may probably have lived in Moulton).

The William of this period may have been Adam's brother. In 1354 John Assheton, parson of Davenham, Randol Roter, William Bostock and Robert Mascy of Sale, entered into a recognizance as sureties for the profits of lands known as *Chirchemosse* (in Davenham). On 30 September 1361, a William Bostock was appointed by the Black Prince as steward of the manor of Frodsham and was still acting as such in 1363 when he occurs with a David Bostock, perhaps another brother (see below), and Richard Bret of Davenham in a recognizance of 20 marks payable to the Earl, regarding a fine of £40 owed by Randol Roter.[2] This fine is interesting. It was paid as a consequence of the killing of Robert Frodsham at Newton by Frodsham, on 29 April 1362, by William Bunbury, a servant to David Bostock. Forcible help had been given to Bunbury by Randol Roter, junior, David Bostock, Richard Bostock and others. It is very likely that William, David and Richard were brothers. Twenty years later, there was a dispute between members of the Venables family of Kinderton and William Bostock (along with a Brereton and a Wheelock) concerning twenty messuages and nearly 900 acres of lands in Kingsley, Norley, Weaverham, Acton, Crowton, Frodsham and Heswall. This dispute no doubt arose due to William's position as steward of Frodsham. On 3 March 1366, William Bostock was a witness at an inquiry held in Middlewich into the lands held by John Ward of Bostock: other witnesses were Adam Bostock, senior, Adam Bostock, junior, and David Bostock. The same year William acquired lands in Marlston cum Lache, near Chester, through his wife Joan, for which dower he had to sue the prioress of Chester who was then in possession of the property. In 1370, William acquired lands in Bradwall, near Sandbach, and from hereon a branch settled in that township.

Pedigrees that mention William seem to give him three marriages: to a daughter of Sir Richard Winnington; to Alice, daughter and heiress of William de Moulton; and to Joan, daughter of the Norris family of Speke and widow of Sir Thomas Daniers of Tabley, a renowned campaigner of the Hundred Years War who had died in 1354. The *Visitation of Berkshire* says that he was knighted by King Edward III on one of the campaigns into France but there is no evidence of this. William died in 1387 in which year his widow sued for dower lands in Wimboldsley. He seems to have had a son named William, for when he was appointed to the post of steward of Frodsham in 1361 he was described as 'senior'. His son may have been the William Bostock who in 1366 was under-seneschal to the abbot of Vale Royal.

Burke's *Landed Gentry* also says that William was knighted by King Edward III and lists other children: Robert Bostock of Warmingham, who married and had issue who lived in that area (i.e. John who occurs in 1435 as deputy for the lord of that manor); Ralph Bostock, the head of a family which settled in Moulton for many generations; David Bostock; William Bostock, the under-seneschal of Frodsham, who had sons John Bostock, lord of Worleston (near Nantwich), and Thomas, both of whom were archers in the service of the Crown in 1398.

William's brother David, referred to above, occurs in the years 1364 and 1374. He had a son also named David who in 1398 occurs as an archer of the crown and a member of King Richard II's bodyguard, and another son, John, similarly described. One of these Davids may have settled at Churton in the west of the county though some pedigrees suggest a David of a later generation. David, junior, accompanied King Richard to Ireland in 1399 and had 'letters of protection', issued on 8 June, which names Thomas Brett of Davenham as his attorney.[8] Another brother was Ralph Bostock who, in 1344, was named as the father of William, a monk at Vale Royal Abbey.

ADAM III BOSTOCK (C.1335-1372)

The next generation of the main line has, as lord of the manor, Adam Bostock, who is for the purposes of this work Adam III. From here on the descent of the main line is more certain. Adam was probably born about 1330-1335. He is rarely found in contemporary documents, perhaps because he spent much time on military service in France and Spain. An Adam Bostock is known to have served in Gascony in 1356/7 and may have served at the famous

English victory fought at Poitiers. On 26 May 1357, an order was issued to the Black Prince's administrators in Cheshire stating that the Prince had granted Adam a life-time release from performing certain services on behalf of the Prince, *viz.* leading beasts seized for debt to Middlewich for onward transport to Chester Castle. Others who held tenements in the township of Bostock were still required to perform this service.

According to Piers Leycester's pedigree, Adam was knighted by the Prince of Wales at the battle of Najera which was fought in Spain on July 1367. If this is so he served alongside the famous Cheshire hero of the Hundred Years Wars, Sir Hugh Calveley, whose marvellous effigy is to be seen at Bunbury parish church.[2]

Adam married Margaret, a daughter and co-heiress of Sir John Wettenhall, alias Kingsley, lord of Wettenhall, Acton and Dorfold. She and her sisters were declared heirs on the death of their brother Richard Wettenhall, the last surviving male representative, who died childless in 1370. The other daughters married into the families of Arderne, Hinckley and Manley. At the time of her brother's death Margaret was herself already dead; as the other daughters were then aged about twenty-one she must have died young.

Adam also did not live to any great age for his *inquisition post mortem* was taken in 1373.[10] It recorded that he died on Friday, 26 February 1372, and tells us that he held a house and grounds with one ploughland in 'Little Stanthurle' (Little Stanthorne) valued at 46*s* 8*d* a year, and that he had granted the manor of Bostock, held from the St Pierre family, to the vicars of Davenham and Weaverham in trust until his eight years old son, Adam, reached the age of twenty-four. A proviso stated that Adam's brothers William and David would succeed to the manor should the young Adam die early. The manor was valued at 60 marks (£40) a year. A fresh inquisition held in 1387 recorded that Adam III, on the day he died, held the manor of Bostock from Walter de Cockseyne of Kidderminster who had inherited the lordship through an heiress of the St. Pierre family: Adam was then aged at least twenty years old.

Most of the pedigrees that have been published of the Bostock family show Adam and Margaret as having five male children: Adam IV, David, Thomas, Richard and Nicholas, all born between about 1363, when Adam IV was born, and 1370, when their mother died: as Adam lived for only a further four or five years this left the children orphaned. It is possible that one or two of the children quoted in the pedigrees may have been brothers of Adam III rather than his sons as the wording of the inquisition and the succession to the estate being in favour of Adam's brothers William and David, suggests that Adam

III died leaving only one son: had there been other sons the manor would have been passed to them each in turn rather than being 'entailed' to the uncles.

Of those who were probably brothers the following may be true. David Bostock married an heiress of the Dee family and founded a family that settled at Churton. William Bostock resided at Huntingdon and had a son also named William who in 1433 was said to be sixty years of age and husband of Alice de Mulneton whose daughter and heiress married a member of the Cotgreave family. Thomas Bostock was an archer of the 'Livery of the Crown' in the service of Richard II in 1398 who, in that same year, gave evidence against the Abbot of Vale Royal on a charge of impoverishing the Abbey's lands. Richard Bostock, described as armiger (esquire) in 1398 was later styled 'Sir Richard' when he received an annuity from the king for his services. He had sons William, who had letters of protection in 1394, and Richard who, in that same year, became a monk at Vale Royal: Sir Richard died in 1417. Another Richard, styled 'junior' was in King Henry V's retinue in that same year. Nicholas, who appears in Ormerod's pedigree, lived at Mobberley and had a son John who maybe the man who served as an archer with William de la Pole, duke of Suffolk in November 1436.

Before leaving this generation it is worth repeating the facts of Adam III's parentage. All pedigrees state that he was son of a William de Bostock, but available evidence suggests that this is not so. Adam de Bostock (III) who held the manor from the heirs of the St. Pierre family according to the inquisition of 1372 was, according to the document of 1354, son of Adam (II) who was son of Adam (I) whose widow Matilda sued John de St. Pierre, her husband's lord, for dower in 1350. A succession, therefore, of three first-born sons named Adam who were lords of the manor of Bostock.

ADAM IV BOSTOCK (1363-1414)

The next lord of Bostock was also named Adam. There is some evidence as to this Adam's year of birth as, according to his father's *inquisition post mortem*, he was eight years old in February 1372. The major piece of evidence as to his age is the *prob etat* (proof of age) taken at Middlewich on 17 September 1385, meaning that he had attained his 21st birthday a short time before. It was most important that an heir's proper age be determined in order for him to prove that he was legally able to inherit his late father's estates and to be free of the constraints of wardship. To prove the age, evidence was given before a jury of local men: Randle Legh, Richard Leftwich, William Warmingham, John Bulklegh, John Leighton, Thomas Brett, Richard Scott, John Littleover,

Randle Wever, William Wever, Hugh Dandy and Thomas Clive. A second inquiry was held 26 February 1387 as regards his inheritance in Wettenhall.[11]

The evidence given stated that Adam, son and heir of Adam Bostock, was born at Bostock on 14 August 1363 and that he was baptised in Davenham church. Randle Legh was the first and principal witness and from his evidence we know something of Adam's childhood. Having been left as an eight years old orphan he was placed by the earl of Chester under the guardianship of Sir William Legh (perhaps of Bageley) and lived with his kinsman Randle Legh. In that household he would have been taught the necessary skills required of a young man of those days and have received a basic education. By the age of sixteen, when his education would have been complete, he was placed in the wardship of Henry Bradshaw of Bradshaw, Lancashire, who then arranged Adam's marriage to his own daughter Janet (quite the usual thing for guardians to do). According to an account of the Bostock genealogy written in 1498 she was styled 'the Lady of Mosley', presumably alluding to one of her father's estates.[12]

Adam Bostock as he might have appered in armour, based on the effigy of his colleague's father, Ralph Davenport in Astbury Church

Adam's career is perhaps the most interesting of any of the family during the Middle Ages. In 1386, he is mentioned as nephew and co-heir of Richard Wettenhall of Acton and Dorfold, who was lord of those places and others around Nantwich, and in possession of 'Sparrowgrove' in Elton and lands in Warmingham parish. The other co-heirs at this time were Henry Ardern and Richard Manley who had also married sisters of Richard Wettenhall. In 1394, Adam Bostock and Richard Manley occur in a writ concerning damage done by their enclosure of lands, contrary to the forest laws, in the Forest of

Mondrem (the southern half of what we now know as Delamere which then extended from Frodsham down almost as far as Nantwich and would have included the township and manor of Wettenhall).[13]

In 1395, Adam pursued a feud with Stephen, abbot of Vale Royal, whose lands at Darnhall bordered Wettenhall. Both men were bound over in the sum of £200 to keep the peace on two separate occasions: Sir Ralph Vernon and David Bostock stood as sureties for Adam. The following year an inquiry was held into the damage, waste and impoverishment of the abbey's lands, for which Abbot Stephen was held to account. The following persons gave evidence on oath: Adam Bostock, Thomas Shaw, Ralph Wever, Hamon Bostock, Richard Wrenbury, Thomas Halghton, Thomas Lostock and Ralph Pulle (Poole). In 1396 the sheriff of Cheshire was ordered to produce before the justices the following members of the family: Adam, John son of William, Thomas son of Adam, Hamo, David of Christleton, and to arrest John and Thomas concerning the death of a servant of the Abbot of Vale Royal: Hamon and David were to respond as regards aiding and counselling the death.[14] Hamon Bostock was a man who saw service in France with the legendary Sir Hugh Calveley in the retinue of Thomas Woodstock, duke of Gloucester, on campaign in June 1380

Adam was a faithful supporter of King Richard II and became one of the captains of his bodyguard with forty-four men under his command of whom six were members of the Bostock family. He was first recruited on 10 October 1397 with an annuity of 100s a year for life.[15] He then had a further annuity of £20 a year.[16] Overall the royal bodyguard consisted of hand-picked Cheshire men who were split into six watches, the captains of which were: Thomas de Beeston, Richard de Cholmondeley, Ralph de Davenport (whose father's effigy lies in Astbury church), Thomas Holford, John Legh and Adam Bostock. The men of these watches were described by contemporaries as 'arrogant, insolent ruffians, who were on far too intimate terms with the King' and as 'bestial men who were ready for any iniquity'. The archers who formed the guard wore a uniform of green and white tunics, divided vertically, with green to the wearer's right – a traditional form of clothing for Cheshire archers.

In addition to the personal guard, Richard recruited an army of Cheshire men during 1397 and 1398 in order to challenge those who opposed his rule. A large detachment recruited by Richard's favourite, Robert Vere, was routed on its way to London at Radcot Bridge in December 1397. It is possible that members of the Bostock family were in that army, though their names do not appear in the lists of one hundred and fourteen men who received compensation for injuries received in the skirmish.

During the last few years of Richard's reign the army and bodyguard were strengthened and amongst those recruited we have the following Bostocks:

Thomas, son of John, recruited on 14 December 1397
William, 15 December 1397
Thomas, son of William 13 December 1397
John, 15 December 1397
Thomas, son of Adam 7 January 1398
John, son of David 30 January 1398

The following received annuities of 100 shillings for life:

David of Churton, on 1 February 1398
Richard, armiger, on 29 May 1398

David son of David had the king's letters of protection on departing for Ireland, which were dated 8 June 1399.[17]

On 17 September 1397, King Richard used his Cheshire archers to overawe the high court of Parliament in order that it would yield to his personal direction; some even nocked their arrows within the precincts of Westminster Hall. Some of the family may have escorted one of Richard's leading opponents, the earl of Arundel, to execution on Tower Hill. The royal bodyguard followed Richard and his court everywhere and remained with him until the end when, in 1399, Henry Bolingbroke captured him on returning from Ireland. The King constantly rewarded his captains and we find Adam receiving £20 a year in 1398 and then in October of that year a half share of £200 due from the assets seized from a man who had escaped custody.

In 1397 Adam occurs as a surety for John de Davenham, canon of Vale Royal, who was charged with a breach of the peace. Earlier the same year he, along with Hugh Bostock, William le Roter and John de Dyseworth, entered into a recognizance of £146 13s. 4d. to Margaret wife of John de Grendon.

These were lawless times and the description of King Richard's archers as being 'ruffians' may not be far from the truth. Members of the Bostock clan were certainly involved in violence at this time as evidenced by the incidents with Vale Royal Abbey. Hugh son of Adam was indicted for a felony in 1384 and fined 13s 4d for shooting arrows at John son of David Bostock at Bostock and wounding him – something of a family squabble which leaves us wondering what it might have been about.[18] Earlier the same John had been indicted for an assault in Wincham.[19] A William son of Richard Bostock, servant to John de Bulkeley of Eaton, was accused of striking a man with a stick in Moulton and was fined 13s.[20]

The *Visitation of Berkshire* says that Adam was knighted by King Richard but the contemporary documents call him 'esquire'. Despite his allegiance to King Richard, Adam seems to have fared well enough under King Henry IV. In 1400, he and John de Wheelock had command of sixteen archers, as part of a contingent of sixty raised in the Northwich Hundred, for an expedition to Scotland in July of that year.[21] When Henry Percy raised the banner of revolt in 1405 Adam, like other ex-members of the late king's bodyguard, followed suit and at the battle of Shrewsbury, 20 July 1405, Adam had command of a unit. After the rebels were defeated Henry IV formerly pardoned the men of Cheshire on 27 September, but Adam and four others, former captains of the old guard, were especially excluded.[22] Each of them had to make special arrangements to sue for their pardons and to encourage them to do so their properties were declared forfeit. Despite a writ ordering seizure of his lands dated 7 October 1405, Adam did not seem to suffer. Not so lucky were his neighbours, Sir Richard Vernon of Shipbrook and Sir Richard Venables of Kinderton, who were executed three days after the battle and had their bodies displayed on the gates of Chester as an example to any who treasured the memory of Richard II.

Adam began to prosper under the Lancastrian kings. The *Visitation of Berkshire* referred to before, says that Adam was visited at his home by King Henry IV and granted the antelope crest which the family used from this time on. It is possible that the use of the antelope occurred at this time as King Henry did use such a badge which could be then borne by retainers and adherents in the form of a cognizance or livery badge. He obtained confirmation of his annuity of £20 that had been granted by the late king and in 1404 and 1406 he was commissioned to lead men to the Welsh borders to help quell unrest in the Principality. In this latter year Adam occurs in a lawsuit brought by William Venables of Kinderton concerning the wardship of Richard son of John Wheelock. Adam and others were accused of having custody of young Richard, his sixteen messuages, a mill, and 452 acres which John Wheelock had held of William Venables by knight's service. Presumably Adam was acting as the boy's unofficial guardian - the jury found in favour of William Venables. In November 1408, Adam, with others, acted as an attorney for John Kingsley during his absence from the county.[23] Then in 1412 Adam and his son, Ralph, were at Macclesfield church to witness the settlement of a feud between the families of Robert Legh of Adlington and Sir Thomas Grosvenor of Eaton.

Adam died on Monday, 12 March 1414, aged about 50, his son and heir, Ralph, then being aged at least twenty-three. His *inquisition post mortem* was heard at Middlewich on 28 March. It recorded that he held a moiety of the manor of Wettenhall directly from the king as earl of Chester by military service and that it was worth £20 a year. He held the manor of Bostock worth £20 a year from Hugh, son of Walter de Cokesay, by virtue of military service, and also that he held the manor of Huxley, worth 13 marks, from Roger Hokenhull by other services. In Tattenhall, he had a messuage, 24 acres of land and a water-mill worth five marks; in Christleton, two messuages and twenty-one acres in worth 15s 4d, from the abbey of Dieulacres, and two messuages and 43 acres worth 6s from Chester Abbey; in Newton by Tattenhall sixteen acres of woodland, worth 13s 4d; in Tetton a messuage, 43 acres of land and 6 acres of woodland worth 53s 6d., from William Trussel, lord of Warmingham; in Occlestone two messuages and fifty-six acres of land, worth 56s from Sir John Ardern; and in Monks Coppenhall a messuage and thirty acres of land worth 15s held from Lord Lovell. The total valuation of his lands was £65 5s 2d.

According to a pedigree compiled in 1498, Adam III and his wife Janet (Bradshaw) had a very large family of nineteen children.[23] Only three sons and three daughters are actually recorded in the document: Ralph; Hugh, who died without issue; Henry (who married Alice, daughter of Thomas Brett of Davenham, whose descendents settled at Middlewich and Huxley); Margaret (who married firstly Hugh Davenport of Henbury and secondly Thomas Staveley; Elizabeth (who died unmarried); and Anne (whom Ormerod calls Agnes). Ormerod also adds another son named William, who is said to have resided at Huntingdon and married Alice Milton, but here I think Ormerod is mistaken and this William is of an earlier generation (*see above*). Mention has already been made of another son Thomas: in 1407/8, a Thomas Bostock of Bostock and others were sureties for a Gruffydd Wright who was contracted to repair the bridge in Northwich. It is also likely that Adam had a son named David who resided at Christleton in view of his ownership of property there. The son Hugh may be the same man as the one who served in John Talbot's retinue at Rouen in 1436 and at Dieppe six years later, when Talbot was created Earl of Shrewsbury.

Before moving on to the next generation of the family other Bostock entries from contemporary documents may be mentioned. In 1432/3, a Nicholas Bostock, then aged 47 years, recited that in 1411/12 he, with others who were of a similar age, went to London in company with Sir Ranulph de Mainwaring who had been ordered to attend the king's council to answer for certain offences he had committed.[24] Nicholas is probably the brother of Adam III who settled at Mobberley. His son John, along with Randle Baskerville and his wife Agnes, levied a fine in respect of two messuages, 100 acres of land, four acres of meadow and two of wood in Mobberley and Werford, in 1461/2. A William Bostock was at Tomberlaine, north-east France, as an archer under Thomas Burgh in June 1428; mustered at Chartres, France, on 16 January 1430, for service with Sir Robert Hungerford; and on 28 September 1437 was a member of a detachment of the Rouen garrison and was at the siege of Tankerville, Normandy, with the earl of Shrewsbury. It is known that a Laurence Bostock served in Aquitaine under Sir Robert Clifton in the retinue of John Holland, duke of Exeter in June 1439. According to the *Visitation of Herefordshire* 1569 he was a knight and a third 'brother of Bostock' who had a daughter named Joan who married a Sir Roger Minors but nothing else is known of 'Sir Laurence Bostock'.[25]Another source places this marriage in the reign of King Henry III or Edward I.[26]

REFERENCES AND NOTES FOR CHAPTER TWO

The majority of the information provided comes from Ormerod's *History of Cheshire*, vol iii.

1. Burke's *Landed Gentry*, in the pedigree of Bostock of Sittingbourne. This fact is also mentioned in the pedigree of the Bostocks of Abingdon in the *Four Visitations of Berkshire, 1532, 1566 1623, 1665-6*, Harleian Society, vol. LVII (1908)
2. This basically means that the men administered the town on behalf of the Earl of Chester, paying him a set amount each year and then making profit from any rents and other dues collected.
3. 'Advowries' were places in Cheshire where fugitives from English justice might seek sanctuary on payment of a fee. The system of 'advowry' was introduced by the Norman Earls of Chester to increase the numbers of men available for military service.
4. Medieval rights of free use of the mill's hopper and freedom from other tolls concerning use of the lord's mill - be it water mill or windmill.

5. Use of the mill.

6. *The Black Prince's Register*, vol. iii, pp. 148, 160. Booth, P.H.W., and Carr, A.D., (eds.), 'Account of Master John de Burnham the Younger, Chamberlain of Chester', *Record Society of Lancashire and Cheshire, vol. CXXV* (1991), p. 121.

7. A medieval mark was worth 13s 4d, therefore 20 marks equals £6 13s 4d

8. 'Letters of protection' were documents affording a person protection from litigation whilst abroad on royal service.

9. *Register of Edward Prince of Wales*, vol. III. See also Bostocks of Abingdon in the *Four Visitations of Berkshire.*

10. *Ormerod, vol. III, p. 254.*

11. *Ibid.*

12. *Calendar of Recognisance Rolls of the Palatine of Chester (C.C.R), Deputy Keeper's Report, vol. 37, p. 45*

13. *Public Record Office (PRO), Chest. 26/9, m.31.*

14. *C.C.R, p.45*

15. *Calendar of Patent Rolls 1395-99, p.381*

16. *Ibid, p. 259*

17. *Chest. 38/22-24, m.21d.*

18. *Chest. 38/22-24, m.15.*

19. *Chest. 38/22-24, m.5d.*

20. *PRO, TNA, E101/42/29, m1.*

21. *Rymer's Foedera, vol. 8, pp. 312-333.*

22. *C.C.R., p.45*

23. *C.C.R, p.46; Ormerod, p. 255.*

24. *British Library, Harl. MS. 2059, f.259*

25. *Visitation of Herefordshire 1569*

26. Burke, J., *A Genealogical and Heraldic History of the Commoners of Great Britain*, vol. I, (1834) p.86

2. THE FIFTEENTH CENTURY

Sir Ralph I Bostock (1392-1419)

Ralph Bostock, born in 1392, was the next lord of Bostock. In his youth he was married to a wealthy heiress – Isabel, daughter and heiress of William Lawton of Wigland and heiress of her mother Margaret, heiress of David Wigland who held a share of the barony of Malpas. Through this important marriage the family's fortunes increased considerably as they became possessed of lands in south-west Cheshire, especially around Malpas and in south-east Cheshire around Church Lawton and Alsager.

Ralph spent a great deal of his adult life in military service fighting in France with the armies of Henry V.[1] On 17 July 1415, Ralph, then styled 'esquire' received letters of protection on going to France in the king's retinue. In the Agincourt Roll he is listed as *Monsigneur* so there can be little doubt that he was knighted during the famous campaign, or actually at the battle that was fought on 14 October that year.[2]   In the battle he served under the banner of Sir Richard Hastings in the King's Division. In December, he was styled Sir Ralph when at Harfleur with Thomas Beaufort, duke of Exeter.

In April 1416, Ralph was commissioned to collect 5,000 marks (£3,333) from the Northwich Hundred to help finance a second invasion of France. Then on 9 July, he had 'letters of protection' when about to embark for France with a contingent of archers, once again in the king's retinue. In February 1418, a large number of archers, to be led by fifteen captains, were recruited for service in Normandy. Ralph recruited only seven archers: Richard Croxton, Nicholas Brook, John Dikonson, William Wigland, Thomas Bailey, Richard Wolf and William Hainson. In April of that same year he once again had 'letters of protection', this time stating that he was going to France with the Duke of Exeter and naming John Huxley, David Bostock and others as his attorneys. Ralph may have been at the siege of Rouen which came to a successful conclusion, under the leadership of Exeter, in January 1419.

Ralph is heard of in matters other than military ones. In 1412, a dispute over lands in Pulford and elsewhere led to a feud between the Leghs of Adlington and the Grosvenors of Eaton which was finally resolved at a ceremony in Macclesfield church which was attended by both Ralph and his father: the ceremony was performed after the celebration of Mass before fifty-eight of the Cheshire gentry. In 1419, Ralph Bostock, John Done and others assisted Sir Peter de Dutton to raid the lands of Sir William Atherton. The rioters stole forty oxen, forty cows, assaulted Atherton's servants and damaged property. Atherton later retaliated by seizing the raider's horses and saddles. On 9 April the following year, the dispute was settled by the arbitration of John, Duke of Bedford.

Ralph died as a young man in his late twenties, on 22 January 1419, whilst on active service in France. The date of his death suggests that he died as a result of injuries received during the siege of Rouen, or else of a disease contracted on the campaign. However, the 1498 pedigree of the family states that Sir Ralph died at 'Agyncourt in France', which is clearly not correct, but then later says that he died at 'Harefleet in France', presumably meaning Harfleur.[3] His *inquisition post mortem* was heard that year but much of the document is too defaced to read the list of places where he held lands in right of his wife, but the following we do know. Sir Ralph held the manor of Bostock together with lands in Occlestone, Calveley, Alsager, Moulton and Tetton, two properties and eighty acres in Church Lawton by right of his wife, and half the manor of Wettenhall; all worth £8 6s 8d. His son and heir Adam was then aged seven years.

Through his wife, Ralph inherited lands and salt-pits in Wigland, Malpas, Iscoyd, Agden, Chidlow, Cuddington, Foulwich and Bradley. He may also have had an interest in the mills at Bradley and Oldcastle inherited from David de Wigland. A hundred years later this estate was described as consisting of thirty messuages and 1340 acres, which included 500 acres of wood, 100 acres of marsh and 200 acres of heath, along with a water mill. An inquisition of 1424 recorded that Ralph also held a half of the manor of Wettenhall from the king. By an inquisition dated 1433, it was recorded that Ralph had died seized of all the lands mentioned above and that they had been in the custody of 'the late king' (Henry V) during his heir's (Adam's) minority and that the wardship and marriage of the heir had been granted to John Kingsley, esquire, then the escheator of Chester. It was also stated that the heir was then of full age (*i.e.* at least 21 years old).

Mention has already been made of Sir Ralph's brothers and sisters, but the following extra details are worth mentioning. The sister Margaret may have been older than Ralph by about five years for, in 1405, she was old enough to bear her husband, Hugh Davenport, a son named Thomas. Sister Agnes married Thomas, son of Thomas Brett and brother of Alice Brett, who married Hugh Bostock. There was another sister named Matilda who was the subject of a marriage settlement dated 1402 between her father and Hugh Holme of Middlewich, by which she married Roger Holme. Ralph's brother Henry

Bostock of Huxley had a son named William who was contracted to marry Margery, daughter of Thomas Mason of Middlewich: the contract stipulated that Thomas was to invest the couple with the perpetual rights to all his lands in Middlewich (both Adam IV Bostock and an Adam son of David Bostock witnessed the deed).

Sir Ralph seems to have been survived by only two children: Adam, who became the next lord of the manor, and Hugh, who apparently resided at neighbouring Wharton and occurs in 1434 in an award of arbitration made by Abbot John de Wheathampstead, alias Bostock, abbot of St. Albans.

ADAM V BOSTOCK (1412 - 1475)

According to his *prob etat*, Adam de Bostock, the fifth in this account to be so named, was born at Bostock on, or about, 6 March 1412.[4] The proof of age, taken at Tarporley on 17 April 1433, is a most interesting document. It tells us that the senior member of the jury, William Bostock of Huntingdon, then aged sixty, gave evidence that Adam was aged twenty-one on 5 March 1433 and that he remembered Adam's birth at Bostock and his christening in Davenham church. He knew these facts because he had married Alice Mulneton in the February following Adam's birth and that the details of the marriage were written in the missal at the church. Robert Waryhull, aged 55, and Thomas Bateson, aged 57, agreed and stated that they knew the facts because on the day of the baptism they were with Ranulph Mainwaring at Davenham for a 'love-day' between him and Sir John Carrington. David Bostock, aged 54, Geoffrey Starky, aged 47, Nicholas Brett, aged 60 and Ranulph Bostock, aged 49, also confirmed Adam's age. These men remembered that not long after Adam's birth a Richard Hilmon of Davenham was infected by disease the cause of which was examined in the Coroner's Court. The remaining jurors gave evidence that the details of the birth and baptism were entered in the church missal, they were: Thomas Pennington, aged 45, Hugh Coventry, 50, Richard Burgess, 60, Thomas Swettenham, 54, and Henry Bostock, 60.

It would seem that there can be little doubt that Adam was born in the spring of 1412. Being only seven when his father died, the manor of Bostock and the other lands were seized into the hands of the earl of Chester, by the escheator of Cheshire, John Kingsley. For thirteen years Kingsley farmed the estates and drew on the revenues arising from them; he was also successful in obtaining the guardianship of the young Adam for himself. But Adam did not see eye to eye with his guardian and may have suspected his intentions for, in 1433, there was a feud between them. Problems between the two had started in January that year as on 14 of the month Adam entered into a recognizance in the sum of £200 not to depart out of the inner bailey of Chester castle - a form of detention. Another recognizance dated 28 February was issued for Adam's safe custody. It is possible that Adam, anxious to obtain his patrimony, was rebelling against Kingsley who was holding on to the estates for longer then he should. Adam's *prob etat*, heard on 9 March, was as a result of a petition to the king for livery of his lands. During 1433-4, Adam was bound over to keep the peace towards Kingsley on five separate occasions, in sums ranging from £100 to £200. In his struggles friends and relations including his brother Hugh Bostock and his cousin Hugh Bostock of Hassall assisted him. An award of arbitration between Adam and John Kingsley, dated 11 February 1434, was made before Abbot John of St Albans.[5]

Kingsley was not the only one with whom Adam had disagreements. At the same time as he was in dispute with Kingsley, he feuded with Thomas Hill and George Weaver, and in the following year with Alwed Radcliff. In fact, he appears regularly in various recognizances to keep the peace from 1435 onwards. Despite this apparent lawless behaviour he, along with Hugh de Bostock, Henry de Bostock, and Ralph de Bostok of Bunbury, was commissioned to arrest Henry de Merton and John de Croxton for various offences.

Returning to domestic matters, Adam finally received livery of his lands on 22 April 1434, about the time of his marriage to a neighbour's daughter who was to become a rich heiress. Hugh Venables, baron of Kinderton had two sons: Hugh, who died childless in 1449 and Richard, whose only son, Hugh, was slain at the battle of Bloreheath in 1459 before he could father any children. Old Hugh Venables also had two daughters: Joan, wife of Richard Cotton of Cotton and Ridware, and Elizabeth, who married Adam Bostock. These two daughters eventually became heiresses to the barony of Kinderton, which included the manors of Kinderton, Mershton, Witton, Eccleston and Brereton, with lands in Rostherne, Sproston, Newton (on Wirral), Bradwall, Tetton, Stanthorne, Wharton and elsewhere, along with salt-pits and houses in Middlewich and Northwich.

A few years before Adam came of age, he and his brothers, Hugh and Henry, were named in a document dated 1429/30 as having an inheritance of lands Middlewich, Knutsford, Holmes Chapel and Nantwich, which were settled by Agnes, daughter and heiress of Roger de Holme of Middlewich: it is likely that she was a daughter of their aunt Matilda Bostock who had married Roger Holme.

In 1442/3, Adam acquired eighteen acres of land, an acre of meadow and three acres of woodland in Wygland from Margaret, wife of David de Malpas. These additional lands were probably some part of his mother's inheritance. Six years later, Adam was bound over to keep the peace towards the abbot of Vale Royal on two occasions in the sum of £100: sureties were held by Thomas Bostock, Adam son of David Bostock, Hugh Venables of Agden and William Holford. Three years later he was bound over again, this time in the sum of £200. These sums of money pledged for Adam's good behaviour may not sound a great deal, but in the mid-fifteenth century they were the equivalent of £40,000 and £80,000 in today's money.

Adam saw military service in France and in the winter of 1440 he was serving with Sir Thomas Kyriell in the Calais and Rouen areas.[6] He was involved in military matters at home too when, in the summer of 1456, Henry VI's queen, Margaret of Anjou, and her son Edward, Prince of Wales and Earl of Chester, visited the midlands and the north-west to seek support for the king against Richard Duke of York and his followers. Cheshire was to become her power base and to those she recruited she issued her badge of a white swan. It is somewhat ironic that a Lancastrian king should find support in a county once so loyal to Richard II a little over sixty years before, and whose people loyally wore the badge of the white hart. The rebellion of the Duke of York in 1458/9 began the second phase of the Wars of the Roses. In September 1459, the Queen and her son were based in Chester whilst the king was at Nottingham. Men from all over Cheshire joined the Lancastrian army under the leadership of Lord Audley. Then, on 25 September, the army of Cheshire men blocked the advance of a Yorkist contingent that was travelling from Newcastle to Market Drayton, on their way to meet up with the main army at Ludlow. At Bloreheath the Queen watched the battle from a nearby church tower and witnessed the destruction of her army and the slaying of many Cheshire men. The defeat was in part due to the treachery of Thomas, Lord Stanley, his brother Sir William and their Cheshire contingents. The desertion by the Stanleys cannot have been a last minute decision for there is evidence of their hindering recruitment for the Lancastrian cause on the Wirral.

The ancient pedigrees of the family state that a Sir Adam de Bostock was slain at Bloreheath, along with other notable Cheshire men: such as Sir John Done of Utkinton, Sir Thomas Dutton and his sons, Sir John Egerton, Sir John Legh of Booths, Sir William Troutbeck and Sir Hugh Venables of Kinderton. However, as an Adam occurs in later records it seems he wasn't slain in the battle. It is possible that this Adam had a son also named Adam who was the person killed at the battle and, owing to the fact that he died aged about 25 and without children, has been missed by the historians. A clue to such a suggestion appears in Adam's *inquisition post mortem* of 1475 which recorded that the heir was Ralph and added the words 'now surviving as son and heir'; wording that seems to imply there had been another and elder son who did not survive. Indeed, there was another son, but not a legitimate son, a genealogy written in 1498 names a bastard son born to a lady named Ellen who was also christened Adam (see below). It is possible that Adam and his son Ralph continued to support the Lancastrian cause for in August 1462, just over a year after the Yorkists came to power, the two men were bound over, in the sum of £300 to be loyal to the new King Edward IV. Sureties for their allegiance were found with Sir Thomas Manley, Sir John Done and Sir Hugh Calveley.

Between 1434 and 1462 Adam occurs often in contemporary documents and often styled 'armiger' (esquire). On many occasions he was bound over to keep the peace with sureties being found by Sir Thomas Manley, members of the Rotor family, and others, but, after appearing in 1465 as a collector of a subsidy in the Northwich Hundred, he abruptly disappears until the date of his inquisition thirteen years later. In addition to his military and lawless activities Adam is found in connection with the administration of the salt industry in Middlewich. Between 1456 and 1460, he was the farmer of the town for an annual payment of £17 6s 8d payable to the earl of Chester.[7]

On 9 June 1458, Adam was granted a license enabling him to place with trustees nine messuages, six crofts and 450 acres of land, and a rent of four shillings from property in Wettenhall on behalf of Ralph and his wife, Elizabeth, the daughter and heiress of Sir Thomas Dutton of Dutton: a marriage intended to bring the family further wealth. This is in all probability a part of the marriage contract and it should be noted that Ralph would have been about eighteen years old at the time and his wife about ten years old - child marriages were the norm at this time.

Adam died on Sunday, 30 April 1475. His *inquisition post mortem* is very brief and states that on the day he died he only held lands in Occlestone and Calveley and that his 'surviving' son and heir, Ralph, was then aged 30 years; however this age seems to be an error for other evidence suggest he would have been about 35.[8] In her widowhood Elizabeth married a Thomas Skivren.

In addition to the conjectured Adam slain at Bloreheath, there is some confusion over Adam's legitimate and illegitimate issue. According to Ormerod, Adam's children by Elizabeth (Venables) were: Ralph (his heir); William of Stapleford; Nicholas of Mobberley; John of Belgrave; Eleanor, wife of Humphrey Bostock of Moreton Say, Salop; Margaret, wife of Wiliiam Whitney of Whitney; Elizabeth, wife of John Gateacre of Gateacre, Liverpool; and Margery, wife of Lewis Eaton of Wildmore. The heralds in the *Visitation of 1580* give something similar: Ralph (the heir of Bostock); William (of Bostock); Nicholas of Mobberley; Margaret (Whitney); Margery (Eaton); Jane who married Sir Edward Holt (of Wimboldsley); Elizabeth (Gateacre); and Ellen (Bostock). The herald William Smith, Rouge Dragon Pursuivant of Arms, adds illegitimate daughters Emma (who married a Freeston) and Jane (who married a Bostock of Churton). The 1498 document mentioned earlier gives more detail and due to its having been written whilst some of the people named were still alive it has some credibility. This records that Adam Bostock and Elizabeth had two sons, Ralph and William, and eight daughters.[2] It gives the eldest daughter as Jane (Holt); then Eleanor (Bostock) who married for a second time to Thomas Ayton, uncle of Lewis Ayton, esquire, of Ayton in Wildmore, Shropshire; Margaret (Whitney); Elizabeth(Gateacre); and last, Margery (Ayton). Apparently Adam had illegitimate children: by a lady named Ellen (who went on to marry Thomas Crackett of Middlewich) he had a son named Adam, and by a 'Dustomes Bradshaghe' of Middlewich he had: John (who married Margaret Peover of Middlewich); Arthur (unmarried in 1498); along with Jane and Emme who were mentioned by Smith. The marriage of illegitimate Jane is corroborated by the Bostock of Churton pedigree (*see Chapter 7*).

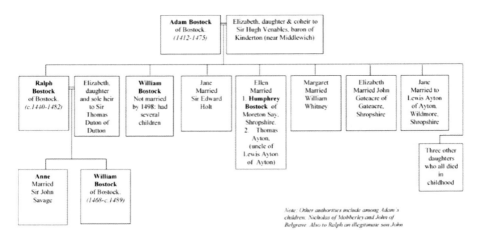

Adam Bostock's legitimate children

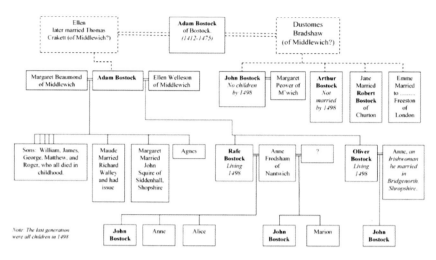

Adam Bostock's illegitimate family

As regards Adam's legitimate son William, who would have been born sometime in the mid-1440s, once again there is some confusion. According to Ormerod he resided at Stapleford (either Fulk Stapleford or Bruen Stapleford, both near Chester) and married Elizabeth, daughter and heiress of Robert Done of Utkinton: a fact confirmed by the pedigree of that family in the *Visitation of 1580*. However, according to the Bostock pedigree in that visitation this William had fifteen illegitimate children, who remained in the Bostock area, of whom only eight are named in the version printed by the Harleian Society. This accords with Laurence Bostock who says he had eight sons and seven daughters all of whom were illegitimate.[10] The 1498 genealogical document says that William didn't marry but by that time had several children. Of these illegitimate, children Edward and Elizabeth were born to an Alice Patrick. George, Ralph, Arthur and Humphrey (who died in childhood), Margery, Emme and Isabel were born to Ellen Bostock, daughter of 'black' Adam Bostock of North Hill, Bostock: none of these nine children were married in 1498 and were presumably children at the time of writing. If William did have any more, as the *Visitation of 1580* would suggest, their being unnamed is to be regretted as a number of families claim decent from this William. A big question now to be posed is: who is 'black' Adam Bostock of North Hill? At the time of writing the question remains unanswered. The modern Bostock Green Farm is on the site of North Hill.

RALPH II BOSTOCK (C.1439 – 1482)

The next generation has a Ralph Bostock as lord of the manor. There is no 'proof of age' for him, but it would seem that he was born circa 1440 as he was said to be aged 20 at the time of his marriage settlement in June 1458, and inquisitions relating to the Venables estate return his age as 20 in 1459. He married Elizabeth Dutton who was about eight years younger and betrothed to him when aged nine or ten: she was a daughter and one of the heirs to Sir Thomas Dutton of Dutton.

During the first year of the Yorkist reign (1461/2), Ralph was bound over to be loyal to the new king in the sum of 500 marks; his sureties were members of the Manley, Calveley and Done families. In the following year he occurs with his father in a similar recognizance. Despite being on the wrong side at the start of his military career, he eventually did well by serving the House of York. It is likely that Ralph fought at the battle of Hedgeley Moor on 25 April 1464 as he had been in the King's service in the north some years earlier. On 3 January 1464, a licence had been issued to Ralph and Richard Cotton 'in consideration of the services done by them at their own costs in northern parts in the retinue of the king and that of Richard earl of Warwick, to enter upon their shares of the manors, lands, etc., of which Hugh Venables died seized of in the county of Chester'. Ralph may have remained in the north to fight also at Hexham on 13 May, and at the sieges of the castles of Alnwick, Dustanburgh and Bamburgh. According to the pedigree in *Landed Gentry*, Ralph fought at the battle of Barnet, on 12 April 1471, and may have been knighted there; he may also have fought at Tewksbury, 6 May 1471, as in both actions it is known that there were contingents of Cheshire men.

The Venables inheritance was to cause serious feuds between the families of Cotton, Venables and Bostock, and their respective allies, for many years. Although Richard Cotton and Ralph Bostock were found to be heirs to the barony, much of the estates passed to a junior line of the Venables family. On 10 May 1466, Richard Cotton, Anne Bostock and William Venables were discharged of their recognizances to keep the peace, 'entered into by them pending a claim to the manor of Kynderton', by virtue of a warrant issued to the Chamberlain of Chester. On 10 February 1467, Sir William Brereton (one of Bostock's trustees) and Ralph Bostock were bound over in the sum of £1000 to keep the peace towards Henry Venables and William son of Thomas Venables of Chester. On a half-dozen times between then and 1469 there are many recognizances and counter-recognizances to keep the peace. In 1471/2 and 1472/3, Ralph and Sir William are again bound over in £1000 to keep the peace towards William Venables of Kinderton and Peter Venables. Brereton alone occurs in similar recognizances over the next several years.

On 20 September 1480, another license was issued to Ralph to enter the barony of Kinderton, as a reward for further services in the north 'as well about the person of the King as that of Richard earl of Warwick'. This, naturally, gave rise to further feuding. Ralph and Richard Cotton were in possession of their shares until Henry, William and Peter Venables put them out by force. Whereupon Brereton prayed for the king's letters to have the rioters put in prison, and him in possession of the estates as guardian of Bostock and Cotton. The title was not settled even then and was to be the subject of litigation for a further fifty years.

In November 1571, Laurence Bostock records that Ralph mortgaged some of his property to William Bulkley of Eyton deputy Chief Justice Chester (1390-1465) for the sum of 100 marks. The property listed was 'The Innhouse called Lawton Yate in Church Lawton, tenements in Alsager, a house in Bostock, a house in Moulton and a house in Wales which was part of the manor of Wigmore'. The property was to be held by the Justice until their return was required by the family on repayment of the capital. Justice Bulkeley then passed the lands on to his daughter Petronilla Brett of Davenham who passed it to her nephew Arthur Holford of Davenham. A John Holford later surrendered the property to Sir John Savage during Queen Mary's reign (1553-4) for the 100 marks.[11]

The death of forty-two years old Ralph de Bostock in 1482 heralds the end of the main line of the family. A *writ de diem* was issued on 20 August 1482, which stated that he had died two weeks earlier; it is said he died from poison, but whether by accident, suicide or murder is not known. His *inquisition post mortem* informs us that he held the manor of Bostock directly from the Earl Chester and that it was worth £10 3s a year. He also held lands in Norcroft, Tetton, Newton by Sydenhall, and Huxley, along with the manor of Wigland, lands in Foulwich, Bradley and Occlestone, half the manor of Marston, lands in Barnton, Legh, Newton (on Wirral) and Northwich. His son and heir was named as thirteen years old William.

Elizabeth Bostock (née Dutton) outlived her husband by thirty-four years. She died in February 1516 and her *inquisition post mortem* recorded that she was in possession of lands in Huxley, Occlestone and Wettenhall granted by her husband as dower. She also held dower lands in Wigland, Malpas, Iscoyd, Agdon, Chidlow, Cuddington and Foulwich which after her death, by virtue of by a settlement dated 1515, were to pass to either her grandson Sir John Savage, husband of Anne Bostock, or else her son William Bostock.

All the ancient pedigrees state that Ralph de Bostock had another son named John who was illegitimate and therefore could not inherit his father's estates; he was said to be the great-grandfather of the antiquary Laurence Bostock (see Chapter 5).[12] This John is an interesting person as according to Laurence and other sources, he was knighted and married a daughter of a wealthy Flemish nobleman – Dame Mary, daughter of Seigneur Henry de Borsalia, count of Grantpré and lord of Vere. Given his antecedents, this John would have been born in the late 1440s, several years after Ralph, and therefore was possibly one of his brothers, not his son: more will be said of 'Sir John Bostock' in Chapter 5.

One of the Harleian documents is the only source which adds a further aspect to Ralph Bostock's family with a family tree showing, in addition to William and Anne, seven others: Ralph, Edward, Reginald, Adam, David, Hugh and Robert, and states that they were all buried in St Stephen's Chapel, Westminster, without leaving any children, except William who had four sons and five daughters - all illegitimate.[13] Interestingly the 1498 genealogy of the family only mentions William and Anne as children of Ralph and does not mention these other sons - perhaps they were already dead. Why were the family in Westminster? Were they performing service of some kind in the capital? Had some sort of plague wiped the brothers out? And what of William's own death at a young age - why and how? St Stephen's, Westminster, was the church in which King Edward IV's body lay in state for eight days following his death on 9 April 1483.

WILLIAM BOSTOCK (1468-C.1489)

But what of Ralph's son William? According to his proof of age, taken at Tarvin on 15 October 1489, he was born on 9 October 1468. Thirteen men gave evidence on the matter before the escheator of Chester: Ralph Daven of Calveley, Thomas Crewe of Wimbalds Trafford, Thomas Rotor and Ralph Littleover, each aged over 50 years, stated that they held torches and candles in Little Budworth church at the time of William's baptism and that the celebration details were entered into the missal of the church. Thomas Hulse of Eton, Robert and Richard Cotgreave, John Dodd of Broxton and Ralph Done of Crowton, all aged 40 years, agreed as to William's age and said that they were in the company of Sir William Stanley and William de Bostock of Wimboldsley, when they were asked to be godfathers to William. Robert

Bostock, John Hankey of Churton, Thomas Done and Thomas Bellet, each aged 30 years, also gave evidence.

In 1488 William was bound over to keep the peace towards his kinsman William Holt, with sureties held by William Kinsey, Robert Bostock and others, in the sum of £100. Holt was bound over to keep the peace towards William in the same sum, his surety being Thomas Venables of Agden. This dispute between neighbours may have had something to do with the old Venables/Bostock feud or else a dispute over property boundaries. The Holt family had held lands in Wimboldsley since the time of King John and at this time held the manor of Wimboldsley and lands in Sutton and Occlestone from Thomas Stanley of Aldford, with other lands in Holt and Newton (both on the outskirts of Middlewich) from Sir James Tochet. The Bostocks also held their lands in Wimboldsley and Occlestone from the lords of Aldford and earlier in the century the Occlestone lands had been described as two messuages and fifty-six acres of land.

About the time of William's *prob etat* we hear of him acting as a trustee and feoffee of Ralph Vernon of Haslington and having custody of that manor. This is an interesting fact as a family of Bostocks settled in the village about this time or a little later. Otherwise, the records are silent concerning William Bostock. The pedigree in Burke's *Landed Gentry* states that William died unmarried in 1487: this cannot be correct in-view of proof of age having been taken in 1489. Presumably he died shortly after and was buried, as already mentioned, in Westminster unmarried and without any issue.

Curiously, William Smith, the herald, in a large pedigree of the Bostock family shows William as having married an unnamed daughter of the Booth family from Dunham Massey and proceeds to show a family descended from him. This has to be a gross mistake by Smith for why would the Savage family have inherited the Bostock estates through William's sister - that can only have happened when there was no surviving, direct, legitimate male heir to the Bostock line. The family he then shows descending from this William is the one normally associated with the illegitimate issue of his uncle William (Ralph's brother).[14] The College of Arms must have been convinced by this alleged descent as they allowed the remaining Bostocks to quarter the Dutton arms which ought only to be used by the direct descendants of Ralph II and Elizabeth Dutton. Perhaps Smith was trying to show that his mother who was a member of this branch was of legitimate stock. Also, surprisingly, Smith makes no mention of the mysterious 'Sir John Bostock', William's half-brother.

The Effigy of Anne Bostock's Husband, Sir John Savage VI, in Macclesfield Parish Church

The main line of the Bostocks of Bostock has come to an end, succeeded by the Savage family as lords of the manor of Bostock - a family which rose to become Viscounts Savage, Viscounts Colchester and Earl Rivers. Anne Bostock's husband John Savage was knighted in 1497 and was sheriff of Worcester for a total of 24 years. He died on 2 March 1527 and was buried in Macclesfield church where the armoured effigies of members of his family can be seen.[15] When the next Sir John died, his son an heir, another John, was still a minor and so Sir William Brereton of Malpas received from the Crown the wardship of the heir and a lease of the Savage estates. Sir William then married young Savage's widow, Elizabeth, a daughter of Charles, earl of Worcester, who was Henry VIII's cousin and his Lord Chamberlain. Brereton and his wife therefore had full control of the Savage estates, including the manor of Bostock, until 1536 when he was executed for treason by virtue of an alleged affair with King Henry's wife, Anne Boleyn.

There are no known monuments to any of the medieval members of the Bostock family within the county. However it is known that there was an inscription with the painting of an achievement of arms to the memory of Ralph Bostock in the parish church of Church Minshull. Sampson Erdswick recorded this in 1572, along with another fifty or so to be found on the walls and windows of the church, but none of these have survived.

The Bostock family did not disappear from the area for a few families of the name continue in the district around the ancient village for many generations. These are the subjects of the following chapters. Branches of the family also settled in many places around the county at Tattenhall, Huxley, Churton, Woodhead, Congleton and Macclesfield, as well as at Holt, Denbighshire, Moreton Say, Salop, and Abingdon, Berkshire - these will be the subject of later chapters.

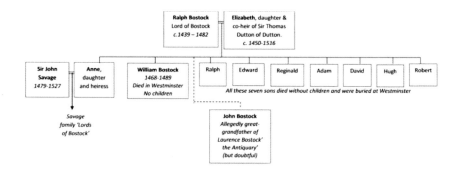

The End of the Main Line
(Based on Harl MS. 245)

THE GENEALOGY OF 1498

There have been several references to the written genealogy of 1498 and it is perhaps appropriate to consider some further aspects of it, as it is seemingly a credible document. It is also very important in that it introduces family members not mentioned elsewhere and males who may have gone on to produce any number of different branches of the family.

On 3 May 1576, Laurence Bostock, the antiquary, obtained from a fellow Cheshireman, Phillip Oldfield, attorney of Grey's Inn, London, an old book of pedigrees that had been found in a student's room in Oxford: the authorship is unknown. The pedigrees, which seem to have been compiled in the latter months of 1498, were made for the 'howse and Family of Bostok in the Countie palentyne of Chester'.[16] Laurence then made a 'true copy' on 14 June 1580 before delivering the original into the keeping of Robert Glover, then Somerset Herald of Arms, who probably referred to parts of it in compiling his *Visitation of Cheshire* that year.

Laurence's copy covers several sheets of text and describes the family that settled in Middlewich and Huxley along with its connection to the ancient line of Bostock of Bostock and begins by listing the heads of the later generations of the medieval family: Adam, Sir Ralph, Adam, Ralph and William. The Middlewich and Huxley lines descend from Henry Bostock, Sir Ralph's brother. It is particularly revealing as regards the numerous children born to some generations and the names of many bastard children and their mothers. In compiling the record the pages are placed out of order and makes reference to the fact that the genealogy begins on page 259, with an introduction at the bottom of page 258, continues on page 260 before returning to page 251 and then continuing through to page 255. Between pages 256 and 258 the descent of the Middlewich and Huxley families are dealt with.

REFERENCES AND NOTES FOR CHAPTER THREE

The majority of the information provided comes from Ormerod's *History of Cheshire*, vol. iii. and from the Harleian manuscripts in the British Library.

1. Ormerod, III, p.255
2. Harl. 782, f.83
3. Harl. 2059, ff.255,259
4. Ormerod, III, p.255
5. The arbitration award is copied in R. Chignall Bostock's booklet on the history of the Bostocks of Tarporley published in 1903.
6. PRO, TNA, C76/123, ms. 32, 38. CPR 1436-41, p.507.
7. As 'farmer' he held the rents and profits of the industry, the markets and courts, on payment of a set annual sum; any surplus was his profit.
8. Ormerod, p.256
9. Harl. 2059, f.259
10. Harl. 245, f.165v. It should be noted that Smith makes a fundamental error in drafting his pedigree as he associates this William's family with the William son of Ralph and brother of Ann Savage who it is known died without any children before 1498.
11. Harl. 245, f.165
12. Harl. 2075
13. Harl. 245, f. 165v
14. Harl. 1500, f.24
15. The effigies are mentioned in Bostock, T., *Cheshire's Monuments to the Past 1. Medieval Effigies* (2016)
16. Harleian MS. 2059, ff. 255-259.

3.   THE TUDOR PERIOD

The last chapter took the family as far as the end of the fifteenth century and into the start of the Tudor period of English history. One might expect information about the family to be somewhat clearly in the sixteenth century but, after the demise of the main line of the Bostock family after a period of three hundred years as 'lords of Bostock', a number of families of the name continued to live either in Bostock or one of the neighbouring towns of Middlewich, Stanthorne, Wimboldsley, Wharton, Moulton, Davenham, Shipbrook, Whatcroft, Leftwich, and Northwich. Throughout the Tudor and Stuart periods there seems to have been some movement of the families amongst these places and it is difficult, despite entries in the parish registers and various wills, to follow their genealogies. The regular use of Ralph, William, Arthur and Thomas as first names adds to the confusion. More importantly it is not easy to assess which of these families was the more senior line - each seemingly being able to stake a claim. For the modern family historian linking to these families, and thus to the main line, is a frustrating task – impossible in most cases.

In considering the family's continuance in the area there are a few contemporary records: the Muster Roll of 1545; the Subsidy Rolls of 1545 and 1559; an undated rent roll of the Barony of Shipbrook; occasional lists of freeholders in the Northwich Hundred; the *Visitation of Cheshire* held in 1580; the papers of Laurence Bostock and his contemporary the herald, William Smith, Rouge Dragon Pursuivant of Arms; and the account books of Sir William Brereton of Malpas, who had custody of the barony of Shipbrook about 1530. All of which are held in either the Public Record Office or the British Library.

MUSTER SUBSIDY AND FREEHOLDER ROLLS

The Muster Roll of 1548 is a list of those aged between sixteen and sixty who were liable for military service.[1] Men had to attend the muster, with whatever equipment they might have, where their names were recorded. The lists were compiled by township and give information about a man's ability and availability. Thus, we have listed for the Northwich Hundred the following adult Bostock members.

> *John Bostock of Elton, a billman*[2]
> *Henry Bostock of Northwich, a billman, lacking harness*

George Bostock of Witton, a billman, lacking harness
Laurence Bostock of Bostock, a billman, lacking harness
Robert Bostock of Bostock, a billman, lacking harness
John Bostock of Bostock, a billman, with harness
Adam Bostock of Bostock, a billman, with harness
Ralph Bostock of Moulton, unable to serve

What is not clear from the muster roll is who were members of the same household, for it is quite possible for a father and son, or sons, to have been eligible at the same time. This roll can be compared with the Subsidy Roll of the following year. Granted by Parliament in December 1545 for two years, rates were to be charged on moveable goods worth over £5, and land worth more than 20 shillings a year.[4] Assessments were to be made by 12 February and certified by 10 March 1546 and 1547 with payments due at the Exchequer by 1 April in both years. In the Northwich Hundred the following members of the Bostock family are recorded:

Arthur Bostock, in goods, worth £9.   paid 6s.
William Bostock, in land worth, 40s.   paid 4s.
Adam Bostock, in land, 26s. 8d.   paid 2s. 8d.
Ralph Bostock, in goods, £5   paid 3s.   4d.

The first three resided in Bostock and the last in Moulton. No other person with the surname are recorded elsewhere within the Hundred but it is possible that there were a few other men whose wealth in terms of goods and land did not meet the criteria; for example, there is no mention of Laurence or of Henry.

Fifteen years later the Commons granted another subsidy to be levied over two years. Assessments had to be made by the end of April and payments were due by the end of June.[5] Only two Bostock families are listed:

William Bostock, senr. in land, 20s   paid 16d.
William Bostock, junr. in land, 20s.   paid 16d.
Ralph Bostock in land, £4 5s.   paid 4d.

Once again the first two men lived in Bostock and the third in Moulton. Again it is possible there were others who fell below the criteria of £5 in goods or 20*s* worth of land. At an unknown date in the mid-16th century the following are listed as living in Bostock according to a rent roll for the Barony of Shipbrook, which at that time did not include Moulton:

William Bostock, William Bostock 'of Sparrow Green',
Thomas Bostock,
Robert Bostock,
William son of Henry.

Robert and William were freeholders of the barony and perhaps resided on land held for many generations.[6] About 1560 the following freeholders were listed:

> *William Bostock of Bostock,*
> *Henry Bostock of Bostock,*
> *Ralph Bostock of Moulton.*[7]

Eighteen years later in another list William Bostock is omitted and had perhaps died by then, in fact Henry died the following year.[8] The information gained from the above sources suggests that there were, in the mid-16th century, three or four distinct families residing in Bostock and one in neighbouring Moulton. The registers of St Wilfrid's church, Davenham, suggest that only four families were flourishing in the 1560s-1570s, those of: Henry, William, Edward and Robert Bostock.[9] The question is how do they link to the original main line of the family? What follows is an attempt to unravel the mystery.

THE FAMILY OF THE VISITATION, 1580

A pedigree of the family is recorded in the *Visitation of Cheshire* compiled in 1580 by Robert Glover, Somerset Herald and published in 1869 by the Harleian Society.[10] This records a family of Bostocks of Bostock and Norcroft (a hamlet in the township of Occlestone) that descended from the same William Bostock who it says fathered fifteen illegitimate children, though the pedigree only quotes eight of them. This William, born about 1445-50, is often styled a 'of Stapleford' and is crucial to the continuance of Bostock families living in Bostock. He may also be the William Bostock 'of Wimboldsley' (a township which borders Occlestone) who was present in 1468 at the baptism of William, the last of the line of the lords of the manor, and if so his uncle. William seems to have died before 1530 as his 'widow' Ellen was allowed 25 shillings a year for the rest of her life, the cost of her rent for her home in Bostock. This entry in all probably relates to Ellen Bostock, daughter of 'black' Adam Bostock of North Hill, Bostock, who was mother to George, Ralph, Arthur and Humphrey (who died in childhood). Annuities of £3 were paid from the issues of lands in Occlestone, to George Bostock, and his brothers Ralph and Arthur, which had originally been granted to each of them for their life-times by Sir John Savage, the husband of Anne Bostock.

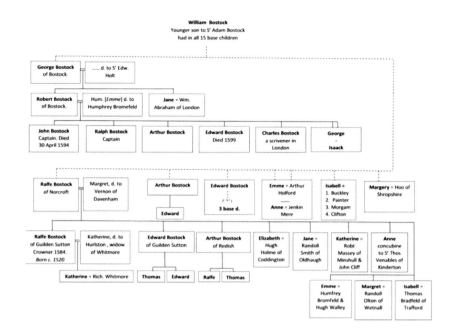

The Bostocks of Bostock and Norcroft from the Visitation of Cheshire 1580.
(Dotted lines indicate illegitimate children)

William Bostock's eldest illegitimate son is shown as George Bostock of Bostock who apparently married a daughter of Sir Edward Holt (a family that lived in Wimboldsley). She may also have been a cousin, as his aunt Jane married, for a second time, Sir Edward Holt. The pedigree in the *Visitation* mentions George's brothers as: Ralph of Norcroft; Arthur, who had a son Edward; and Edward, who had three illegitimate daughters. George's sisters were: Emme, who married Arthur Holford; Anne, who married Jenkin de Mere; Isabel, who had four husbands – Buckley, Painter, Morgan and Clifton; and Margery, who married a man named Hoo from Shropshire. The herald Smith agrees with these marriages. The alleged fourth son Edward Bostock (born *c.*1480) was in the retinue of Sir John Savage and his son, the next Sir John (d.1528), who, in March 1516, attacked and mortally wounded John Pauncefote, esquire, a Justice of the Peace for Worcestershire, at Tirley in Gloucestershire, on his way to court.[11] Following suitable payments to the Crown and to the widow, a pardon was issued to the Savage family and their confederates. It seems that George, Ralph and Arthur Bostock served the Savage family in some capacity for a considerable time as they were in receipt of life-time annuities from Sir John.[12] In the Brereton accounts there is also mention of a messuage in Bostock held by Roger Painter – is he one of Isabel's four husbands? Interestingly, an Arthur Painter died in 1573 and his will refers to a debt of 6s 8d owed by his cousin 'Edward Bostock of Bostock'. Perhaps not a coincidence.

The Holt family of George's wife is the same family which feuded with William Bostock, the last of the main line of the family. The last of the Holt family was William de Holt who lost his manors of Wimboldsley and Lea to George Cotton by virtue of an award of the Prince of Wales' council. The Cottons then sold their lands, which comprised of two houses and 60 acres of land in Stanthorne and Wimboldsley, to Sir William Brereton of Malpas in 1545. This parcel of lands may have included the area known as Norcroft where George's brother Ralph lived.

George's brother Arthur in all probability is the same person who left a will dated July 1560 and was buried at Davenham on 3 September. He calls himself Arthur Bostock of Bostock and he held the manor of Morley in Barrow (near Chester) where his brother Ralph was the bailiff to Sir John Savage. In his will he refers to his illegitimate children, William and Jane, and a legitimate son named Edward, as well as Alice, his wife, and a Ralph son of Thomas Bostock, deceased.

According to the family tree drawn in 1580, George had two children: Robert and Jane, who married a William Abraham of London. Nothing is known of Robert Bostock of Bostock other than that he at some time swore to uphold the customs of Davenham parish before the Bishop of Chester, and, therefore, may have been a parish official. He was buried at Davenham on 19 March 1584. According to the *Visitation* he left seven sons: John, Ralph, Arthur, Edward, Charles, George and Issac, but, according to the Davenham parish registers, which began in 1553, he may have had a number of other children, many of whom died young. Three daughters are known to have survived as they are mentioned in their brother's will dated 1594: Elizabeth, Katherine and Eleanor. There is a problem with deciphering the registers at this time as the family of Robert Bostock of Moulton are also listed without any mention of place of residence to identify either Robert. Robert's wife, Emme, was buried at Witton on 30 November 1604, when she was described as 'late wife of Bostock of Bostock': she was a daughter of Humphrey Bromfield of Northwich.

It does seem that Robert's children all lived in London. His eldest son John, born about 1550, is styled 'Captain' and it is known that he was a professional soldier and that he fought at one time in the Low Countries. An indenture dated

14 March 1577, describes John as 'late of London, son of Robert Bostock, the elder, of Bostock'. By this deed, made with Sir John Savage VIII (d.1597), John paid £40 for a 21 years lease on two messuages and tenements lying in Bostock, at a rent of 53s a year. One of the messuages had been occupied by his father Robert and 'lately' by George, his grandfather, and the other by a Humphrey Okes. The lease was to take effect following the death of John's mother Emme. Seventy years later the property was occupied by Thomas Bostock and consisted of 104 acres.[13]

John Bostock of Bostock died on 30 April 1594. His will, dated 16 April that year, survives and provides some useful details of his family. To his mother, Emme, John gave his 'great gilt standinge Cupp of silver with the Cover' and to her and to three of his sisters, Elizabeth, Katherine and Hellinor, he bequeathed all money owed him by a Mr. Cotton and any other person in Cheshire. To his brother Ralph he left his 'messuage or mansion house' in the parish of Davenham together with all its appurtenances, 'estate, right and title and interest', held on a twenty-one years lease following his mother's death. Ralph also received John's best suit of clothes, best gown and cloak, buff jerkin with gold lace, best rapier and dagger, and his gold signet ring. Arthur, his second brother, received John's second suit of clothes, second gown and cloak, a rapier and dagger and a 'Frenche boulle'. Edward also received a French bowl as well as similar items of attire and weapons. Brother Charles had another French bowl and six silver spoons. The remaining brothers, George and Issac, also each received a bowl. Sister Abram, inherited a silver salt cellar and six silver spoons. Abram is an unusual name and may be a surname as John's aunt had married a William Abraham of London and Arthur Painter's will referred to before mentions the same man. His nephew Stephen, son of his sister received £5. The will goes on to mention his good friend Mrs. Crowshawe who was to have his ring set with a diamond, and her two daughters, Katherine and Mary who were to have £20 which their father owed him. Cousin Knowles was pardoned a debt of £8 and she was also to receive one 'Jewell of Ambergrise'. To his cousin William Bromfield he gave five pounds. His two men, James and Walter, each received £5, and James was also to receive a debt of £3, owed by a certain John Haines of Dover in order that he might pay the surgeon 'for his time'. Captain John Bostock had an illegitimate daughter named Tymothy who received £10. The poor people of 'all Saintes Stayminge' in London and the poor of Davenham parish benefited from John's will as the total sum of £20 was divided between them. A total of £40 was to be spent on a 'decent and seemly' funeral. Anything left after all his debts had been paid was to be divided between, Ralph, Arthur, Edward, Charles, George, Issac and Abram. His executor was his brother Charles, and brother Ralph and his good friend Mr. Croshawe were to be his overseers, each of these had to see that his will was carried out so that there was no discord between any of his brothers and sisters. A 'french boull' seems to have been left out of the earlier bequests and as an afterthought it was given to Ralph. The will, which was proved on 23 January 1597, is particularly useful in naming his brothers and sisters and supporting the evidence of the *Visitation*. Three years later a codicil added that if Ralph died then the estate in Bostock was to pass to Arthur the next brother.[14]

Ralph Bostock, second son of Robert was John's heir; he is also styled 'Captain' in the *Visitation* but nothing is known of his career. He left a will dated 20 August1605 in which he is styled 'of the City of London, gent.' His brothers Arthur and Charles were named as executors. Interestingly he mentioned another two brothers 'but I will give them nothing but I utterly disclaim them' - a serious rift between siblings and a comment that is perhaps reminiscent of John Bostock's will in which he asked for no discord between his brothers and sisters. Ralph mentions his sister-in-law, Charles' wife, and uses a nickname 'Mall'. The third son, Arthur, who was baptised on 18 March 1561, may be the father of an Ellen who married Michael Elliot, an apothecary of London, who is mentioned in a visitation of the City in 1633: he is described then as Arthur Bostock of Bostock Hall. He is probably the same as Captain Arthur Bostock, gentleman, whose memorial brass once lay in Dartford parish church, Kent. Although he lived in Dartford he also had property in Newham and a house in Fleet Street, which he leased from St Bartholomew's Hospital. He married Frances Rogers and had one son and three daughters: he died in 1613. In his will is he left a gold ring each for his brother Charles and his wife, and to his other brother Isaac he left twenty shillings a year for life.[15] According to the *Visitation of Cheshire*, the fourth son, Edward, who was baptised at Davenham on 30 August 1562, died in 1599. Issac's baptism is recorded at Davenham on 23 October 1569 and that by 1588 he was an apprentice in London and a freeman of the city nine years later.

Of John's brother Charles, who was born about 1567, we know more as his family is recorded in the *Visitation of London, 1633*, and he appears several times in the records of the Scrivener's Company in London. He was apprenticed to a Roger Bouthe of London in 1575 as a 'scrivenor' (a writer who copied official documents) when he was aged about eight years old. He later lived in Broad Street, London, with his wife Mary, daughter of Thomas

Saunders, a merchant of London, and their five children: Charles, Arthur, Mary, Susan (wife of William Prescot) and Elizabeth (wife of John Rogers, perhaps a cousin). Daughter Mary married Thomas Clowes 'milliner to Queenes Ma'ty ano 1633', son of Anthony Clowes of London and Nantwich. In June 1628, Sir Arthur Savage sold a property known as Bacon House in Oat Lane, London, to Charles Bostock who was acting on behalf of the Scriveners' Company, which then became their headquarters. One of his apprentices was a Giles Bostock, son of William Bostock of Sevenoaks, Kent, a carpenter who may have been related in some way.[16]

The achievement of arms allowed by the heralds is interesting as the quarterings given for Charles' family number twenty. Those numbered sixteen to nineteen stem from the marriage of Ralph de Bostock (1440-1482) to Alice Dutton, suggesting a descent from that marriage. It seems therefore that the heralds had relied upon William Smith's pedigree which does indeed show such a family line from William Bostock son of Ralph and Alice. This is quite erroneous as William died without any children leaving his sister Anne (Savage) as heir.

BOSTOCK OF NORCROFT.

Returning to the *Visitation of Cheshire*. This also records a family that settled at Norcroft, a tenement in Occlestone, near Middlewich. Ralph Bostock, given as the second illegitimate son of William Bostock, is said to have married a Margaret Vernon of Davenham. He seems to be the same person as Ralph who was the Savage family's bailiff for the manor of Barrow in the late 1520s and early 30s. Ralph and his wife had ten children: Ralph, Edward (who lived at Guilden Sutton near Chester and had two sons, Thomas and Edward)[17], Arthur (see below), Elizabeth, Jane, Katherine, Anne, Emme, Margaret, and lastly Isabel. The eldest daughter, Elizabeth married Hugh Holme of Coddington and had a daughter Maud who married a distant cousin - John Bostock of Churton. Randol Smith married the second daughter, Jane, and had a son William, who, in 1609, was appointed 'Rouge Dragon, Pursuivant of Arms' at the College of Arms in London: the same man who has been referred to several times before. He was the author of a treatise on Cheshire and an authority on Cheshire heraldry and may have supervised the painting of the heraldic screens still to be seen in Middlewich church.

In 1531/2, a Ralph Bostock presented an ox, valued at *17s 8d*, to the court of Sir John Savage as a heriot - a form of tax paid to a lord on inheriting an estate on the death of the former tenant.[18]

Ralph Bostock of Norcroft's eldest son, Ralph, married Katherine, daughter of James Hurleston of Chester, and widow of Thomas Whitmore of Caldy who, according to Ormerod, died before September 1553. In 1584 Ralph held the office of 'Coroner' and lived in Guilden Sutton, a village in which the Whitmore family held lands (they also held lands in Thurstaston, Caldy, Tranmole, and, interestingly, Wimboldsley). In 1579, Ralph promised county officials that he would ensure that his daughter Katherine, then wife of her cousin William Whitmore, a tailor of Guilden Sutton, would attend church regularly and take Holy Communion. Before living in Guilden Sutton it is possible that Ralph lived in the neighbouring village of Barrow. A deed dated 6 April 1552, made by John Whitmore of Thurstaston, brother of Thomas Whitmore of Caldy, settled lands on a number of persons of which one was a Ralph Bostock of Barrow, 'gentleman'. These lands were to be held by them for the use of the grantees and the children of this Thomas Whitmore. Ralph also occurs in 1582 when he gave evidence to the Consistory Court to prove the validity of his brother Arthur's will; at that time he said he was aged 63 years, giving him a year of birth of circa 1519. The Bostock families who lived on the Wirral peninsula and around the city of Chester no doubt descend from members of this branch of the family given their connections with Guilden Sutton, Barrow, Thurstaston, Caldy and Picton. Bostock families appear in the parish registers of Broughton, Bebbington and Eastham.

Arthur 'of Redish', seems to be the same as Arthur Bostock 'of Middlewich' who left a will in 1575, witnessed by Eleanor, his wife, his brother, Ralph Bostock, and the vicar of Middlewich.[19] In it he describes himself as 'of Newton, gentleman' (Newton being a part of Middlewich) and mentions his wife Eleanor, and sons Ralph and Thomas who are both shown in the *Visitation*. Ralph was to inherit his father's lands known as 'le Parke' held on lease from Sir John Savage. The validity of the will was proved by Arthur's brother Ralph Bostock 'of Sutton' as mentioned in the last paragraph. Arthur's residence 'Redish Hall' in Newton was surveyed in 1796 when it contained 104 acres, of which almost 25 acres were then newly purchased by its owner John Roylance, esquire. It lies along the banks of the River Wheelock directly across from Norcroft Farm. Until recently the hall and its lands were known as 'Middlewich Manor', but today the whole of the area is a large modern housing development. 'Le Parke' was another area of Newton on the boundary with the townships of Stanthorne and Clive. This family as recorded in the *Visitation* covers a time when the parish registers at Davenham begin - so can the sources of information be reconciled? And, further, does the pedigree tally with other sources? The answer is not an easy one.

There is some difficulty with the registers as the entries do not always give parentage or full details of the mother and father. Also it seems that there were two or three families headed by a Robert Bostock: one or two at Bostock and one at Moulton. The reason I say two in Bostock is that in 1577 John's father Robert is styled 'the elder', implying another adult male of the same name; also the registers seem to suggest this given the number of months between some of those baptised as children of Robert. Also, although there is a 'Johannes fill Robti Bostock' listed as being christened on 23 June 1564, he cannot be the 'Captain John' shown in the Visitation' as that John, 'son of Robert the elder', must have been at least 21 years of age in 1577 when he took on the lease from Sir John Savage.

The first person we come across in the Davenham parish registers is 'Arthurus fillius Roberti Bostock' on 18 March 1561, and then we have 'Edwardus fill Robti Bostock' on 30 August 1562.[20] Each of these entries may refer to those sons mentioned as living in 1580, as is the entry for Charles, baptised on 19 September 1567, which does not give a father's name though it could be the Charles who later lived in London. 'Izacus' baptised on 23 October 1569, would I suggest, given the unusual name, be one of the same family. Does the name Isaac have any bearing on the family's connection with the Abraham family of London - were the Abrahams Jewish?

According to the *Visitation,* Edward, Robert's fourth son, died in 1599. The registers of burials at Davenham do record an Edward on 16 May 1600 - is this the same one and is the Visitation in error? Unless he died elsewhere towards the end of March 1599/1600 (New Year's Day then being 26 March) and his body brought to Davenham for internment in May.

Finally, it is interesting to note that the heralds considered this family of Bostock and their cousins of Norcroft to be the senior line. They were allowed to use the coat of arms of the main line without any mark of difference. The fifteen quarterings in the heraldic achievement all stem from marriage alliances made by the lords of Bostock up to the marriage of Adam de Bostock (1412-1475) to Elizabeth Venables.[21] Such quarterings would fit with a family descended of Adam's second son William, and any mark of cadency would be dropped when the main line came to an end.

Referring back to the brothers John and Ralph who were both described in the *Visitation* as 'Captains'. It may be that the following extracts from a series of documents in the Public Records Office, known as 'The Salisbury Collection', refer to them.

On 28 April 1599, a Captain Bostock served with a company of foot soldiers in Munster.[22] On 17 May 1600, Ralph Bostock wrote to Cecil and said that he had completed sixteen years service in the wars and had become much in debt, therefore, he requested another company of foot or else some other employment. He also requested letters be sent to the Lord Mayor of London nominating him as 'Muster Master' of the City.[24] On 22 April 1602, Captain Ousley wrote to Sir Robert Cecil, Queen Elizabeth's chief counsellor, requesting that he continue in Cork (Ireland) with his 'puisnes' (junior) Captain Bostock.[23] same collection of documents refer, in June 1600, to a Thomas Bostock who served with the Levant Company [25] along with sons and servants named as George Bostock, Abraham Sidale, George Conqueste, and Robert Bostock.[26]

THE FAMILIES OF WILLIAM AND HENRY BOSTOCK

Two more families are those of a William Bostock and a Henry Bostock. These two men are linked in Ormerod's History of Cheshire as brothers, a theory which is followed by Burke's *Landed Gentry* in recording the descent of the Bostock family of Sittingbourne, Kent. Even Ormerod was unsure of the genealogy of the Bostocks at this time and notes:

> '.... The family continued to be represented here (Bostock) in name and blood by an unidentified branch, perhaps springing from William, uncle of the last William Bostock, or from John natural brother of the latter, ... Edwardus Bostok de Bostok gentilmon fil Willi Bostok, occurs in the Plea Rolls, 16 Hen VII (1500/1) but as might be expected the notices are very scanty........ These interesting original evidences are in all probability all that remain in proof of the existence on its soil for some generations longer of the last branch of this knightly house.'

Following this comment there then follows transcripts of what Ormerod's editor, Thomas Helsby, considered to be the relevant *inquisitions post mortem* with a rough pedigree.

Recent research in the Hareian collections of manuscripts in the British Library has produced the following chart.

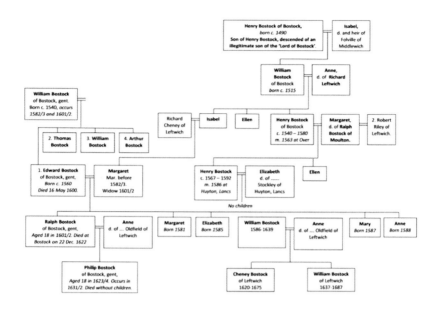

The Bostocks of Bostock according to Harleian MS 139, f. 16 and other evidences.

The version in Ormerod goes back two further generations: William is shown as son of Edward Bostock, who occurred in 1500, along with a suggested brother for him named Roger who occurred at the same time, and they were sons of a William Bostock. In fact, the 'Edward son of William' who occurs in 1500 could well be the same father and son mentioned in the 1489 genealogy and the Roger referred to could well be Roger who died in 1513, son of Henry Bostock of Huxley and Middlewich.[27] Unfortunately those who drafted the pedigree in Burke's Landed Gentry accepted the early part of this family tree.

The pedigree in Burke's adds some extra details without any reference to the source of the information. The William at the head of the chart is stated to be William Bostock, second son to Adam Bostock (1412-1475), but if this were true there is a generation missing. The genealogy copies Ormerod in claiming that William married Elizabeth, daughter and heir of Robert Done of Stapleford, and resided at Stapleford and Wimboldsley and says that couple had sons Edward, with whom the descent continues, and Roger, 'besides fifteen illegitimate children'. Edward of the next generation is said to have lived at Bostock and Whatcroft, and married Anne daughter of John Shaw of Over, and died in 1563, yet the *Visitation* claims he had three 'base' daughters.

In Burke's, Edward's children are given as: William, with whom that genealogy continues; Henry (who is known to have married Margaret, daughter of Ralph Bostock of Moulton at Over, and had two daughters and a son Henry, who died without issue in 1592); Margaret, allegedly the wife of Sir William Cavendish (but see under 'Laurence the Antiquary' for an alternative family connection); Ellen, who died unmarried in 1580; and Isabel, the wife of Richard Cheney. The second William Bostock is then said to have married Anne, daughter of Edward Bulkeley of Moulton and had a number of children, the eldest of whom was an Edward who was born in 1550. This Edward married his cousin Margery Cheney and had issue: Ralph; William (whose family settled at Leftwich and continues the pedigree in Burke's through his son Cheney); Thomas; Margaret; Elizabeth and Anne. Ralph, son of Edward Bostock was baptised at Davenham on 31 July 1583.

An Edward Bostock, presumably William's son had custody of Canterbury Castle during the reign of Queen Mary. During his term of office, in January 1556 he had the custody of Robert Cheney who had committed a 'very notable' murder. The wife of a man named Gibson smuggled a file into the prison with which Cheney managed to escape; somehow he drowned and his body was brought back into the castle and enquiries were made into his escape and eventual death.[28] Being responsible for Cheyney's safe-keeping and perhaps suspected of allowing the escape Edward Bostock was committed to the Marshalsea, the prison of the Queen's Knight Marshal in London. At this time the Knight Marshal was Sir Thomas Holcroft of Vale Royal a few miles away from Edward's home village in Cheshire. A request to free a Christian Gibson was made in May. Was Robert Cheney related to Richard Cheney? What relationship were they to Sir Thomas Cheney, Warden of the Cinque Ports, and what was the nature of Robert's crime. Unfortunately, there is more to this story than we can possibly know.

Whilst the three generations descending from William Bostock can be confirmed by *inquisitions post mortem* and parish registers the rest is speculative, especially the suggestion that William and Henry were brothers. The penultimate generation omits to mention a daughter Mary, who was baptised on 23 June 1587 at a time when her father was living in Wharton, and perhaps another daughter named Elizabeth, baptised on 30 June 1596 (if so, presumably the first Elizabeth died young). The marriage of their father Edward to Margery Cheney occurred on 19 February 1582 which suggests that Edward was born around 1560. His father William may be the man buried at Davenham on 30 July 1563.

Finally, considering the pedigree in the *History of Cheshire* and in *Landed Gentry*, it has to be said that, whilst no doubt correct in some way or another, there is no direct evidence to link the William Bostock at the head of the chart with the William who had fifteen illegitimate children.

The available documentary evidence given by Ormerod says that Edward Bostock had three brothers who are mentioned in his *inquisition post mortem* taken in March 1602. The text of the inquisition states that Edward was a son of William Bostock and his wife Ann, who owned and occupied an 'ancient messuage' in Bostock, and also owned lands there and in Moulton: one of his properties had been occupied by Laurence Bostock, then dead, and then by Edward himself. All these properties were settled on Edward and his wife Margaret, daughter of Isabel Cheney, for life by an indenture dated 1583: failing them having children, the properties were to pass to Edward's brothers Thomas, John and Arthur. According to the inquisition Edward died on 16 May 1600 and according to the Davenham parish registers he was buried the same day. He left a son and heir Ralph, aged '18years 5 months and 5 days' on the day of the inquest. Edward's widow, Margery was buried on 27 July 1602. It is interesting to note the reference to Laurence Bostock, whilst this might be Laurence Bostock 'the Antiquary' mentioned in the next chapter, it is more likely to be a Laurence son of Edward Bostock recorded as being baptised on 3 February 1563.

Ralph Bostock, Edward's heir, married Ann Oldfield of Leftwich, by whom he had a son Philip, born on 30 September 1604. It is difficult to ascertain the names of Ralph's other children from the parish registers as he can be too easily confused with Ralph Bostock of Moulton and his family. Their marriage does not appear in the Davenham registers and neither does the baptism of their son Philip. A baptism of a son Michael, on 4 September 1608, does appear, as does a daughter Mary on 11 January 1618. Ralph Bostock died in 1623 and was buried at Davenham on 22 December. His inquisition states that he held by knights service 'an ancient messuage' in Bostock along with thirty acres of land, meadow and pasture in Bostock and Moulton from Sir Thomas Savage and his mother Mary, and valued at £1. He also owned a 'cottage and curtilage' in Bostock enclosed from the wasteland of the manor that had once been occupied by Laurence Bostock: this was worth 4*d*. Ralph's son and heir was recorded as Philip who was aged 18 on 30 September 1623.

Philip seems to have died without issue, though he may be the Philip Bostock 'istius' (of the same place) who married Frances Minshull of Sandbach on 15 November 1633. He, along with Ralph Bostock of Moulton, witnessed the inquisition post mortem on Richard Bostock of Tattenhall on 18 May 1631. Philip is mentioned on the seating plan of Davenham church which is dated 1635, as is a 'Mistress Bostock' who may be his mother, Ann.

Philip seems to have had some financial difficulties and had to mortgage his estate. In March 1642, he entered into an agreement with Ralph Bostock, junior, of Moulton whereby Ralph agreed to pay Edward Minshull and Philip's other creditors £123 *6s 8d*, and to pay John Mainwaring of Bostock £150 two years after Philip's death. Further it was agreed that Ralph would pay annuities to Philip: £4 for two years and then £8 for the duration of Philip's mother's lifetime along with a single payment of £10 to her. This agreement seems to be tied up with the estate known as 'North Hill House' and fields known as: 'the field at the back of the house', 'Black Acre', the two 'Riddings', 'Malenscroft', the two 'Deanes' and 'Davies Meadow', and a cottage then in the holding of Thomas Oakes. Edward Minshull who is mentioned as one of the creditors was a member of the family which had in 1632 acquired the manor of Bostock, Occlestone, Shipbrook and Leftwich from Thomas, Viscount Savage, and was therefore Philip's landlord. It would seem from this evidence that this branch of the Bostock family resided at North Hill in Bostock and not at the old Bostock Hall as might be supposed. It also suggests that this line of the family were descended of 'Black Adam' Bostock of North Hill mentioned in the 1489 genealogy.

The other leg of this family tree drawn in *The History of Cheshire* has two Henrys in succession, however I do not believe that this part of the family ought to be here as they did not have a common ancestor in Edward Bostock. Certainly the two families became linked when Henry's sister Isabel married Richard Cheney and their daughter married the younger Edward Bostock, but not before that (*see pedigree chart*). A paper amongst the Harleian manuscripts records this particular family and says: 'Henry Bostock descended of a bastard of ye L. of Bostocke marryed Rose d. to Bradshawe co. Lanc.'. In that document the next generation is that of another Henry who married Isabelle, daughter and heiress of the Folville family of Middlewich who had a son named William, who married Anne, daughter of Richard Leftwich of Leftwich. This William 'son of Henry' occurs in a mid-sixteenth century rental of the manors of Shipbrook, Bostock and Shurlach along with another William Bostock and a Robert Bostock.[29] It was William and Ann's son Henry who married Margaret Bostock from Moulton and had a son, Henry, and two daughters.[30] The marriage between Henry and Margaret took place at Over church on 6 December 1563. These last two generations accord with Ormerod's suggested family tree and with information given in *Landed Gentry*. As with William Bostock's family, exactly how Henry's line was related to the lords of Bostock is not known other than having descended of an illegitimate son.

From the Davenham parish registers the following details are available. Henry junior was baptised on 16 September 1567 and daughters Anne on 13 October 1572 and Katherine on 16 July 1578. According to his *inquisition post mortem* dated 1582 he had possession of lands in Bostock and Wharton 'juxta Bostock', held of Sir John Savage manor and worth £1, as well as property in Hatton held from Richard Starkie of Moresalt. In a list of knights, esquires, gentlemen and freeholders of the county made in 1579, 'Henry de Bostock of Bostock, gent.' is listed, as is 'Ralph Bostock of Moulton, gent', but there are no others listed for the area. Henry died on 5 September 1580 leaving a son Henry aged fourteen years. His will dated the same day, mentions his wife, daughters Ann, Katherine and Elizabeth, and sisters Ellen and Isabel Cheney. He held his property in Bostock by virtue of a gift of William Leftwich and reference is made to a lease he had from the Leftwich family dated 4 July 1571 for the lives of himself, his wife and son Henry and of a close called 'High fylde' and a meadow called 'Roger's eye'. Ralph Leftwich, William Marbury and Henry's wife were to hold the estate for the benefit and upbringing of the children. His inventory listed goods worth £84 *17s 6d*. The witnesses were Ralph Leftwich, Edward Bostock, Laurence Marbury and James Marbury. A small codicil concerning some debts was witnessed by Thomas Bostock.

Henry junior married Elizabeth Stockley on 1 January 1589 at Huyton parish church, Lancashire: the baptism of a daughter Margaret occurs there on 15 June 1592. At Davenham the couple had a son, William, baptised in 1590 who died six months later. This Henry held property in Bostock, Wharton, Acton and Hatton. On 12 February 1592, 'Henry Bostock de Bostock, gen.' was buried. He also left a will dated 11 January 1592 which refers to his wife, sisters Elizabeth and Ann, and his mother Margaret, then wife of Robert Ryley of Leftwich. He ordained that should his daughters die without issue then the following were to inherit his estate: Richard Cheney of Leftwich and Thomas Cheyney; Thomas and William, sons of Ralph Leftwich; and Laurence, John, George and James, sons of William Marbury.

A document dated 1663 records the right of title to property in Bostock sold by Sabath Church of Nantwich to Thomas Seagrave of Nantwich.[30] The property was described as 'a capital messuage and tenement with appurtenances situate and lying and beinge in Bostock sometymes in the tenure and holding or occupation of Henry Bostock of Bostock, gent., deceased and his ancestors', and then of Margaret, widow of Edward Church and of Thomas Church; also another messuage in the same place once held by Henry, 'except Roger's Eye'. This Margaret Church is described as being daughter to Edward and Margaret Bostock of Bostock: she married Edward Church in 1639, died six years later, and was buried at Nantwich on 1 September 1645. By 1668, the estate was described as consisting of three messuages, three gardens, three orchards, fifty acres of land, fifteen acres of meadow, fifty acres of pasture and twenty acres of woodland. Seagrave was till in possession of the property when he died in 1676. According to his will he left £15 a year from his estate at Bostock for his wife's benefit whilst the property passed to his daughter Mary and her husband William Hodgkins. The actual ownership of this same property then passed into the hands of a William Derbyshire and then Edward Tomkinson.

To summarise. The families of both William and Henry were not directly linked but were related in as much as they probably descend from one of the many illegitimate sons of the main line of Bostock of Bostock. William's descent is probably from the mysterious 'Black Adam' of North Hill, Bostock. Henry's line may descend from one of the many base sons of William Bostock, second son of the last Adam Bostock (1412 - 1475), though a descent from John Bostock, illegitimate son of Ralph Bostock (c.1439 – 1482), is also a possibility. The truth is we will never know.

REFERENCES AND NOTES FOR CHAPTER FOUR

The sources of information in this chapter have come from a variety of sources. Once again much has been obtained from Ormerod's *History of Cheshire*. Parish registers and wills lodged at the Cheshire Record Office (Cheshire Archives and Local Studies) have also been referred too.

1. Public Record Office (PRO), SP 10/3
2. 'Billman' is an infantry soldier armed with a 'bill' – a pole on which is mounted a curved blade.
3. 'Harness' refers to basic armour – helmet and steel splints to protect the forearms.
4. PRO, E179/86/19
5. PRO, E179/85/57
6. Cheshire Archives and Local Studies (CRO), DCH/I/1
7. Smith W., *The Vale Royal of Cheshire*

8. Irvine, F. (ed.), *Record Society of Lancashire and Cheshire*, vol. 43 (1902)

9. Davenham Parish Registers: burial 5 September 1580.

10. Rylands, J.P (ed.), *The Visitation of Cheshire, 1580*. Harleian Society (1882) and referring to Harl. MSs 1424 & 1505

11. I am indebted to Hugh Savage for this information.

12. E.W.Ives, (ed.), 'Letters and Accounts of William Brereton of Malpas', *Record Society of Lancashire and Cheshire*, vol. cxvi, 1976.

13. CRO., DCH/J/34 & 35

14. Will of John Bostock, National Archives PROB 11/89/595, 11/83/839

15. His will is extant and to be found in the National Archives, London.

16. Steer, F.W. (ed.), 'Scriveners' Company Common Paper 1537-1628 with a continuation to 1678', *London Record Society*, vol. 4 (1968)

17. Thomas, son of Edward of Guilden Sutton, (deceased) had a lease of a messuage, tenement and gardens in Wheelock Street, Middlewich, from William, son of Thomas Venables of Kinderton. The lease, dated June 1579 was for 80 years at an annual rent of 6s 8d. 9d. (CRO: DV1/MV1/23)

18. Ives, *op cit*.

19. CRO: WS

20. I here use the modern calendar. Prior to 1752, a new year would have begun on 1 April.

21. For the significance of the 'quarterings' on the coat of arms see a later chapter.

22. Hist. Mss. Comm. *Salisbury Papers*, ix, pp 145

23. *ibid*, vol. xil, p. 117

24. *ibid*, vol. x, p.149

25. The Levant is the eastern shores of the Mediterranean Sea and includes Turkey, Egypt, Italy, Persia, and) Crete. The Turkey Company, later known as The Levant Company, was probably the most profitable branch of England's overseas trade between from the 1580s up until the 1620s and beyond. In exchange for alum from Italy, the English would trade herring (from the north), tin and lead (used for the war), and their native cloths, especially kerseys.

26. *ibid*, vol. x, p. 216

27. Harl. MS 2075

28. Dasent, J.R. (ed.), *Acts of the Privy Council of England Volume 5, 1554-1556*, (1892), p. 219].

29. Harl. MS 139 f.16

29. CRO: DFN 2705/19 and DTM16

30. CRO: DCH/I/1

5. LAURENCE BOSTOCK'S FAMILY

LAURENCE 'THE ANTIQUARY'

Laurence Bostock, the antiquary, was born about 1520, when King Henry VIII was ruler, and and died in 1580 during the reign of Queen Elizabeth I. He wrote a great deal about the history of Cheshire and its various families; his writings, almost all of which seem to date to the 1570s, are preserved in the British Library, London, among the Harleian Collection. His papers may be divided into a number of classifications: Cheshire history, English history, genealogy and heraldry. He was prolific in accumulating antiquarian material - letters, deeds, inquisitions, pedigrees and heraldic drawings - and in doing so corresponded with many gentry families through the country. His own writings seem to date from no earlier than 1570 and we have no information about him before that. The bulk of material surviving in the PRO are referenced as Harley 139 with 283 items on 260 pages put together in the form of a book which became the property of Sir Simonds d'Ewes (1602-1650) who prefixed the title as follows: *An Excellent Booke concerning most of the Lands, Descents, Coat-Armours, and other passages both Legal Historical, of the County of Chester. Collected, out of Records, Private Evidences, Epitaphes, and divers Other Monuments, by Laurence Bostocke, or, as he calls himself, Laurence of Bostoke.* Of the family descents Laurence mentions, for example, are the families of Audley, Beeston, Brereton, Cotton, Davenport, Dutton, Egerton, Grosvenor, Hatton, Helsby, Mainwaring, Olton, Savage, Starkey, Thornton, Venables, Wetenhall, and of course Bostock. Of a more general historical nature he deals with the Earls of Chester, the baronies of Halton and Shipbrook, the descendants of Llewellyn Prince of Wales, the lords of Powis, and a treatise on *The Peopling of England by the Saxons.* He visited numerous churches and recorded the heraldic monuments he found there: *e.g.* Alderley, Aldford, Audlem, Eccleston, Davenham, Marbury, Mobberley, Pulford, Rostherne, Tarvin, Wrenbury and Wybunbury, as well as the abbey church at Chester and Norton Priory. A particularly interesting paper is a diary of Laurence's journey from London to Cheshire in 1575 which lists the people he met and stayed with, the route he took and the mileage.

Ormerod, in his *History of Cheshire* states that he was the great-grandson of John, the illegitimate son of Ralph de Bostock (1440-1482) a fact he may have obtained from Laurence's own notes: based on likely dates of birth this is unlikely. In 1573, Laurence wrote about his father's and grandfather's military exploits which also gives some details of his family connections, but only covers three generations and misses the vital link with the main line of the family.[1] This pedigree concentrates on Laurence's links with the family of Eton of Eton, Shropshire, and through them the Barrows of Barrow and the Sneyds of Keele. A pedigree Laurence drafted the following year later gives what he considered to be the link with the main line of the family, by stating that his great-grandfather, whom he calls 'Sir John Bostock', was the illegitimate son of Sir Ralph; however, there are some doubts concerning this descent from Ralph given the likely dates of birth for each generation (see below).[2] The family trees lists three Johns in succession which for clarity will be designated John I, John II and John III.

A man named Laurence was buried at Davenham on 31 March 1582: the Davenham parish register describes him as 'senex' - old. If this is the same Laurence he was aged about 62 years.

JOHN I BOSTOCK

One version Laurence's pedigree indicates that John I, called 'Sir John', who would have been born about 1450, was first married to a daughter of Sir John Warburton and had a daughter by her.[3] After this marriage he fled to Flanders with King Edward IV, who is known to have been in exile there with his brother Richard duke of Gloucester, in 1470. A note in red ink adds that 'this John was absent out of England 36 years'. When Edward of York was in exile he lodged with Louis de Bruge, Lord of Gruuthuse, husband of Margaret, a daughter of Henry de Borsalia. In return for his hospitality King Edward later gave Gruuthuse the hereditary title of Earl of Winchester.

Whilst in Flanders John married for a second time to Dame Mary, daughter of Henricke de Borselen (or Borsalia), Count of Grandpré, Lord of Vere and Zandenburg, Vlissingen (Flushing), Wasschappel, Domburg and Brouwer Haven - the most prominent noble family of Zeeland: they were related to the Scottish and French royal families and to the dukes of Burgundy.[4] The van Borselen (Borsele, or Boprsalia) family seat was the castle at Zandenburg, which has a rich history reaching back to the mid-thirteenth century. From 1467, Henricke had the French title of Count, or Earl of Grandpré (in Champagne, France) having purchased that county from its previous owner. He was made a knight of the Order of the Golden Fleece in 1445 and died in 1474. On 26 December 1429, he married firstly Joan of Halewyn, daughter of Olivier of Halewyn, Lord of Heemsrode and they had a number of children of whom the eldest was Wolfart VI. This Wolfart married Mary, King James of

Scotland's daughter and through this marriage became Earl of Buchan: he was also Stadholder (Governor) of Holland, Friesland and Zeeland, Admiral of the Netherlands, from 1478 a knight of the Order of the Fleece and in 1464 Marshal of France: he died in 1487. Wolfart's sister Margaret (d. 1510) married Lewis of Bruges, lord of Gruuthuse, who in 1472 was appointed as Earl of Winchester by King Edward VI in gratitude for the hospitality and support he had offered him when in exile.

The only thing so far known about Henricke de Borselen is recorded in various state papers. On 18 February 1472 the count and officials of the town of Vere issued letters to King Edward IV granting his subjects the right to trade in the town of Vere free from any taxes: this was in return for privileges the king had given them.[5] In November the king issued instructions to the customs officials of London and the main English ports to allow 'Sir Henry de Borsalia, count of Grandpré, lord of Veer, and the burgomasters, scavins, consuls and community of that town' right to import and export goods.[6] The prosperity of the port town of Veere was based on the cloth and wool trade with England and Scotland. From December 1507, a Henricke Borsalen was lord of Lauderdale by the gift of King James IV of Scotland. How John came to make such an important match is not clear but may be linked to the exile of King Edward IV in the winter of 1470/1.[7]

Clearly Laurence claimed a descent from an important match. One of his papers consists of 'Certain notes taken out of the last will and testament of] Henry van Borsalia, Lord of Camphre....'[8] These notes list various religious foundation established by his great-grandfather and then includes a short family tree which includes John Bostock who is called 'Sgr. de Beauce Chattell' - presumably he had custody of the castle. Beneath this he lists the monetary bequests made to Henricke's sons and son-in-law. The next page has notes from a will which seems to be that of Frank II van Borselen, Graaf van Oostervant, written in the town of Brielle in 1466/7. This Frank died on 19 Nov 1470 in Brielle, Zuid-Holland, Netherlands, and had married Jacoba, Duchess of Bavaria, in July 1432. If the copies of the wills were genuine and the bequests to John authentic then 'Sir' John Bostock did indeed make an important match. No doubt he met Mary whilst on military service with King Edward VI in Flanders, given that his wife's sister married the King Edward's host, the lord of Gruuthuse .

In one of the Harleian papers the family tree has a number of sketches of coats of arms. Alongside John is the shield illustrated below. However, these cannot have been arms borne by John as the impaled coat is not that of his father-in-law, but of Wolfsen VI Borselen, his brother-in-law. It is formed from the basic arms of the Bostock family impaling the quarters of the Borselen family. The arms of Borselen and Bostock were by coincidence very similar: a black shield with a silver bar, though for Borsalen the bar was not cut short: the four quarters of the Borselen family include the arms of the earls of Buchan (the three wheatsheaves) and an unidentified coat of arms.

The Arms ascribed to 'Sir John Bostock'
(Based on Harl. MS 2075, fo.44)

JOHN II BOSTOCK

Laurence's grand-father is given as 'John de Bostoke d'nus ib'm armiger' (meaning 'lord of the same, esquire') and his grandmother as Mary, daughter and heir of Roger the heir of Hugh Eton of Eton esquire 'descended of Sir Nicholas Baron of Stockport'. He will have been born about 1470 but what we do not know is whether he was son to the Warburton lady, John's first wife, or to Mary Borsalia - the pedigrees all suggest the later but it is not necessarily the case. According to the military service account written by Laurence, this John was at the sieges of Therouanne and Tournai in August and September 1513. John and Mary are known to have had two children - John and Margaret.

This John (or perhaps his son) occurs in the early sixteenth century records of the Court of Star Chamber.[2] Sir Piers Dutton claimed that on the night of 15 January 1528, John Bostock and William Groves, men 'of evil disposition', broke into a house on the manor of Dutton allegedly on behalf of their master Sir John Savage. The following day Savage and 200 armed men caused an armed riot on other parts of the estate. Savage was in dispute with Sir Piers over the inheritance to the Dutton manor and claimed the estates in right of his mother Ann Bostock heiress of her mother Elizabeth, a Dutton heiress. John

Bostock of Middlewich, was one of those accused of being involved in the armed riot. The outcome so far as the Bostock men are concerned is not recorded but in all likelihood they had to be bound over to keep the peace.

JOHN III BOSTOCK

This John was Laurence's father. Born about 1495, he married Ellen, daughter of Roger Warenne esquire of Ightfield, Shropshire and they had, in addition to Laurence, sons Robert, Matthew, John and Roger and a daughter Alice (who married John Banks of London), all of whom would have been born between 1520 and 1550. Piers Leycester, another seventeenth century antiquarian, says that Laurence's brother, Robert, had a son named George who lived at Calveley.

Laurence's record of his father's military service begins with a reference to the battle of Flodden which was fought on 9 September 1513. Something like a thousand Cheshire men took part in this event which saw the death of King James IV of Scotland. Laurence's father John III and Sir George Holford had command of the Abbot of Vale Royal's contingent of 300 men fighting with the Cheshire troops under the overall command of Sir Edward Stanley on the left wing of the English army. Laurence then says that John was at a battle he calls 'Bromefylde' where King James V 'was slaine'. This seems to refer to the battle of Solway Moss fought on 24 November 1542, for it was after that battle that King James V of Scotland, father of Mary Queen of Scots, died; he didn't actually die at the battle but shortly after, disheartened by the news. The next journey he mentions was to Ireland, under 'good Sir William Brereton' who became Lord Justice of Ireland and is known to have visited Ireland in 1534. Then he mentions the northern rebellion of 1543 and John's service under George Talbot, earl of Shrewsbury. John then served with Sir Hugh Calveley in the punitive expedition that led to the burning of the cities of Leith and Edinburgh in May 1544. For the invasion of that year Cheshire contributed a substantial company of 2,000 archers and billmen, as well as numerous esquires and gentlemen. After Edinburgh, King Henry VIII's brother-in-law, Lord Hertford, dubbed nineteen new knights from the county of Cheshire and several gentlemen were raised to the status of 'esquire', including John's cousin, William Sneyde. In 1547, John, and William Sneyde, were again in Scotland, this time at the battle of Pinkie Cleuch, which was fought near Musselburgh on 10 September (not as Laurence says 15 August). Laurence's father's last adventure was into East Anglia to quell the rebellion led by Robert and William Ket, in 1549, again with Sneyde. After this account Laurence then gives a chart titled the 'descent and genealogy of ye said John Bostoke': it is interesting to note that Laurence considered his father, grandfather and great-grandfather to be 'lords of Bostock'. They can not have been so given that the lordship was in the hands of the Savage family. A John Bostock of Bostock, either this John or his son of the same name, appears in the muster roll of 1548 (see Chapter 4).

Laurence's account is confused. He starts by saying his father was at Flodden and that 'his second voyage or Journay was into Skottland viij years after'. He has the second and third journeys out of order as it ought to be Ireland in 1534 and Scotland in 1542 – eight years later. From then on the chronology is correct. What is little difficult to reconcile is that Laurence's father, when aged about 18 years, had a command of troops at Flodden in September 1513 and was still living in 1574 when Laurence visited him at home in Wistaston - if he was, he was of a great age for those times.[10]

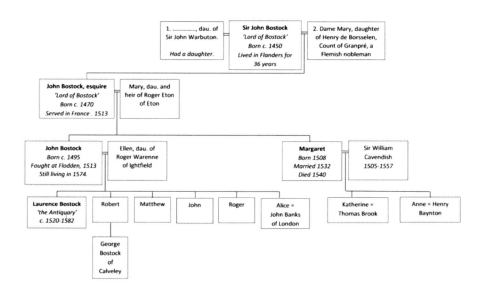

Laurence Bostock's Family Tree.
(Based on Harl. MS 139 & 245.)

THE CAVENDISH FAMILY

Of particular interest is a lady who is shown in one chart as Laurence's aunt. According to the pedigree Margaret married Sir William Cavendish, a well-known Suffolk gentleman and courtier. However, this seems to be false, as most pedigrees and genealogies of the Cavendish family state that Margaret was a daughter to an Edward (or Edmund) Bostock of Whatcroft, esquire, a fact actually recorded in Sir William Cavendish's own notebook which is preserved at Wellbeck Abbey, Nottinghamshire. Margaret was born about 1508, married Cavendish in 1532 and died in Westminster on 9 June 1540, having had five children of whom two girls survived into adulthood - Katherine who married Thomas Brooke, son of Lord Cobham and Ann who married Henry, son of Sir Henry Baynton in 1561. Margaret died on 9 June 1540 and was buried at St Botolph's, Aldgate, London, under the monument to Alice Cavendish, William's mother.

> Here lyeth buried under this stone Margaret Cavendishe late Wife of William Cavendishe, which William was one of the sonnes of the above named Alice Cavendishe, which Margaret dyed the 16 June in the year of our Lord God MCCCCCXL., whos soul Jesu pardon. " Heven blis be here mede Yat lor the sing, prey or rede.

William Cavendish went on to have eleven other children by two other wives. In 1542 he married Elizabeth Parker and had three children by her but none survived, and she died after giving birth to a stillborn daughter in 1546. He then, in 1547, married Elizabeth Talbot, Countess of Shrewsbury (known as Bess of Hardwick). Having sold his property in Suffolk he moved to his wife's native county of Derbyshire and purchased the Chatsworth estate and began to build the well-known Chatsworth House, home to the Duke's of Devonshire.

SOME CONFUSION

Considering the evidence of the military adventures, approximate dates may be given to the generations. If Laurence's father fought at Flodden in 1513 then the youngest he can have then been is sixteen, but in view of the fact that he had a command then I would think he was probably between 18 and 25 years old, giving a year of birth no later than 1493 and suggesting he was in his mid-fifties when he undertook his last adventure in 1549. By computing a generation gap of twenty to twenty-five years, then Laurence's grandfather was born around the years 1465-70 and would have been aged about forty-eight years at the time of the sieges of Therouanne and Tournai in 1513, and, therefore, a contemporary of William de Bostock (1468-c.1515), the last lord of Bostock, and conceivably his brother, albeit a half-brother. However, there is a further generation to consider, Laurence's great-grandfather who married Dame Mary Borsalia, and that John, the first, would have been born around

1445-50 and, therefore, a contemporary of Ralph II Bostock. If John, the natural brother of William, did exist and was Laurence's ancestor then he should be shown as grandfather of Laurence and not a great-grandfather, which then leaves the question of which John Bostock married Dame Mary?

Leycester states that Laurence was the great-grandson of John, an illegitimate son of Ralph's brother William, the third son of Adam Bostock (1412-1475). Leycester also states that Laurence's great-grandparents were: John Bostock and his wife 'Dame Mary, daughter of the earl of Grantsprey (Grantpre) in Champagne and Segnior de Borsalia'. This would of course fit in terms of the number of generations.

REFERENCES AND NOTES FOR CHAPTER FIVE

The majority of the information provided comes from the Harleian manuscripts in the British Library.

1. Harl. MS 139, f.30b
2. Harl. MS 139, f.99v
3. Harl. 245 f. 165v
4. This marriage is mentioned in a number of folios in the Harl. MSs, e.g. Harl. 139, f.99v; 245, f.65v; Harl. 2075, f.43; Harl 1535, f.71.
5. Salisbury, E (ed.) Calendar of the Cecil Papers in Hatfield House, vol 13: Addenda (1915), p. 5
6. Calendar of Close Rolls, Edward IV: volume 2: 1468-1476 (1953), pp 232, 233
7. Letters and Papers, Foreign and Domestic, Henry VIII, volume I: 1509-1514 (1920), pp 82-97
8. Harl. 2059, f. 227
9. Stewart-Brown, R. (ed.) Lancashire and Cheshire Cases in the Court of Star Chamber, Part 1, Record Society (1916), p.87.
10. Harley 2075

6. THE BOSTOCKS OF MOULTON, MIDDLEWICH & LEFTWICH

MOULTON

During the Norman period Moulton was a part of the barony of Shipbrook and had been previously held by a Saxon named Leventot. Whilst this manor was of less value than neighbouring Bostock, having resources that amounted to one hide for taxation and a value of five shillings, its area may have been somewhat larger. There were two ploughlands, one villein, one smallholder with half a ploughland, one acre of meadow, one league square of woodland, and an enclosure for wild animals.[1]

Exactly how the Bostock family became possessed of lands here is not clear. Ormerod states that the first to reside here was Ralph, second son of Sir William Bostock and his wife who was the sole heir of William de Moulton.[2] The *Visitation of Cheshire, 1580*, states that Ralph was 'a younger son' to William de Bostock who had married Alice, daughter and co-heir of Randoll de Moulton.[3] Leycester states that William de Bostock, lord of Bostock, married Jane heiress of the Moultons and that his second son Ralph married Alice daughter and heiress of Randoll de Merton (or Marton). A document in the Harleian collection states that Ralph Bostock of Moulton married an heiress of the Bradford family, who were neighbours of the Mertons.[4] Whatever the truth of the matter the family held lands here before the end of the thirteenth century and also held lands in Marton, Wharton, Shurlach and Stanthorne by the end of the next century.

A little light can be shed on the first Bostock to settle here. In the 1640s William Bostock of Moulton collected together copies of some old charters, the earliest of which, judging by the witnesses named, seems to date to the last decades of the thirteenth century.[5] It states that William Bostock gave to his son Ralph the lands which Warin Vernon held, 2½ acres that Henry Cademan held and four pieces of wasteland lying in longitude between 'the Longlake and the Carter Clough', and in latitude between the hedge of Moulton and the River Weaver. He also gave him pasture rights and other privileges in the township of Moulton. The witnesses included Philip Bostock, Hugh Bostock, John 'clerk of the same place' (Bostock or Moulton?). He was required to pay to his father two shillings a year in equal instalments in February and August, along with other services.

The next copy document is a grant by John, son of Randle de Merton of lands in Moulton to Ralph Bostock and his wife Alice; this is dated 1290 and seems to support Leycester's theory. The property was to pass to Ralph's son William, and should he fail to have male heirs then to the next son Ralph and should he fail to have male heirs then to Ralph's brother Richard, and after him sisters Alice, Matilda, Agatha and Katherine. The witnesses include Adam Bostock. Another three copy documents relate to family property in Moulton, Wharton and Wincham. Other than this, unfortunately, there is little to say of the medieval characters that belong to this family.

As with the main line of the family there are some differing theories as regards the family tree. The heralds' *Visitation* of 1580 has Ralph I succeeded by David Bostock who married a daughter of Sir William Baguley and had three sons Ralph, the eldest, who married a Davenport, Philip who married a Warburton and David who married a Snelston. However, a pedigree drafted by Laurence Bostock has Ralph I succeeded by David who married a 'Weebleton' (Warburton?) followed by Philip followed by Ralph II who married a Davenport.[6] There is some accord with Ralph II having a son David who

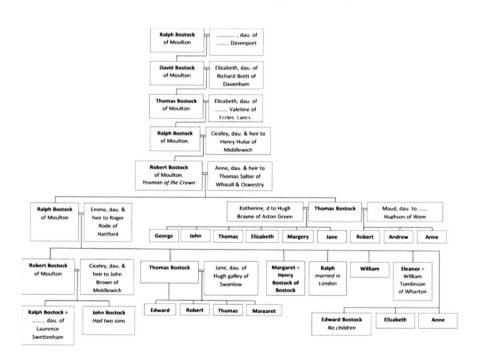

The Bostocks of Moulton down to the early 17th century.
(Based on Harl. MS. 139,245,1535)

married Elizabeth Brett of Davenham, followed by Thomas who married Elizabeth Valentine of Eccles (or Eccleston) of Lancashire, followed by Ralph III.

This last Ralph Bostock of Moulton is said to have contracted a valuable marriage to the daughter and heiress of Henry Hulse, and his wife who was the heiress of the Pickmere family, as a result the Bostocks of Moulton inherited lands in Stapleford and Pickmere. This marriage was celebrated with the the heralds allowing the family to quarter the Hulse and Pickmere arms in their own achievement of arms. In April 1492, an agreement was drawn up with Ralph Bostock that his son Robert should marry Agnes, daughter and heiress of Thomas Salter of Whixhall and Oswestry, who was by then dead: his daughter was in wardship to William and Thomas Tattenhall of Buckley.[7] Following her demise, Robert married Anne Cotton of Whitchurch. From these marriages stem the branches that settled in Shropshire. In 1493 this Ralph was bailiff of Middlewich.

Robert Bostock, described in one source as a 'yeoman of the Crown',[8] died in 1537 and his will, written on 31 March and proved on 9 October, mentions his 'well beloved kinsman and especial friend Raffe Bostocke of Norcrofte'.[9] Robert attempted to leave all his goods to his servant Anne Lowe in recognition of her 'true, diligent and paynefull service' during his 'greate sekenes and contynuell paynes' but it seems that this will was contested as the named executors were excluded and administration of his estate was granted to his widow Anne. He left two sons: Ralph IV and Thomas, who married twice and had children by both wives.

Ralph IV Bostock of Moulton, who eventually succeeded to the family estates, occurs in 1548 and 1552 as a juror on a number of *inquisitions post mortem*. His is the last generation to be recorded in the Visitation of 1580. Ralph Bostock of Moulton and Emme Rode (or Row of Hartford according to Laurence Bostock) had several children: Robert, the son and heir; Thomas, who married Jane Knightley of Swanlow Lane, Over;[10] Edward, a burgess of Middlewich in 1556 and 1565; William; Ellen, wife of William Tomlinson of Wharton; Margaret, wife of Henry Bostock of Bostock; Anne and Elizabeth.[11] Laurence's version adds another son Ralph. Ralph Bostock of Moulton was buried at Davenham on 13 January 1595.

Robert Bostock, born circa 1540, married Cicely, daughter and heiress of John Browne of Middlewich. In 1553 a burgesship in Middlewich was conferred on this John Browne and his heirs – daughters who married a John Reynolds and Robert Bostock, who occur as a burgess in 1556, 1557 and 1565.

However, Robert was barred from continuing in his burgesship on the grounds that he and his wife had murdered Joyce 'late wyffe of John Browne'. The circumstances were that on 9 December 1568, Robert and Cicely, Reynold Duncalfe and Isabel Alexander, all broke into widow Browne's house and that Robert and Reynold strangled the old lady. The two men and Isabel were executed for the offence despite their pleas of innocence and Cicely, being pregnant, was imprisoned for life. At the time of her confinement Cicely again stated her innocence and alleged that those who committed the murder had fled to Ireland. Her appeal, heard by John Throkmorton, Chief Justice of Chester, on 28 February 1571, succeeded and she was pardoned.[12] Letters Patent were issued on 15 January 1574, and then on 14 December 1576, the pardon was again confirmed when Cicely and her new husband, Ranulph Pickmere, were granted a salt-house, two cottages and a garden with all the arrears of the profits, and the restitution of all other goods forfeited since Robert's attainder.[13] It seems that Robert Bostock had been innocent all along. Cicely may have married a third time for there is mention in the Middlewich parish registers of a Cicely Pickmere, 'widow', marrying a James Marsh, clerk, in 1607.

Following Robert's death the surviving trustee of earlier grants, on 11 September 1572, granted Robert's son Ralph V Bostock with the family properties in Middlewich and Newton. The document mentions Robert's other children: William, John and Isabel.[14]

Ralph V Bostock, son of Robert and Cicely, is the first of the family to appear in the Davenham parish registers; he was christened there on 3 June 1567. In 1607 he sold the family's lands in Pickmere to the Starkey family. Ralph may have married twice: firstly to Elinora, daughter of Laurence Swettenham on 14 February 1600, by whom he had no children, and then, Georgina Whalley in 1608. Ralph's eldest son, Ralph, was baptised at Davenham on 23 April 1603. In April 1625, Ralph obtained a lease of a barn and orchard in Middlewich from the Venables family.[15]

In the records of the Cheshire Quarter Sessions there is an interesting case that was heard at Knutsford on 18 October 1642. Ralph Bostock, the younger, of Moulton, delivered articles against his brother Robert. It was alleged that Robert, who was of no fixed abode, was 'dissolute and disorderly', 'very wasteful' and 'given to prodigal and needless expenses' and that due to debt he had fled to Scotland and Ireland. Over the years Ralph had tried to help his brother, by giving him large sums of money, but now Robert was suggesting that Ralph's title to their father's estate was questionable and had threatened to kill him. On 6 September, whilst he was working in the fields, Robert threatened to kill Ralph and struck him with a bill knocking him senseless. Following this incident Robert continued to make threats and constantly carried his bill 'ready sharpened'. The papers continue with evidence that Ralph's wife Ellen was constantly in fear when she left the house, that they were fearful for their six-years old son, and that Robert was also threatening a neighbour, Philip Pritchard of Bostock to whom Ralph had sold a parcel of land known as 'the Tunstalls'. The petition ends with an application for Robert to be brought before the next session, but nothing further is known.[16] Ralph VI Bostock of Moulton, gentleman, was born in 1603 and married Ellen, daughter of John ap Richard (Pritchard) on 25 June 1622. On 18 March 1642, he, styled Ralph 'junior', when he entered into an agreement with Philip Bostock of Bostock concerning lands in Bostock known as: 'Field at back of house, 'Black Acre', the two 'Riddings', 'Malenscroft', the two 'Deanes' and 'Davies Meadow', and a cottage in the holding of Thomas Oakes. Ralph agreed to pay Edward Minshull and Philip's other creditors £123 6s 8d before 20 May, and to pay John Mainwaring of Bostock the sum of £150 two years after Philip's death. Further it was agreed that Ralph would pay annuities to Philip of £4 for two years then £8 for lifetime of Philip's mother, Anne, and to the mother £10 a year. This agreement seems to be bound up with property known as North Hill House in Bostock.

During the Civil War, Ralph Bostock, junior, was a collector of subsidies and rents on behalf of Parliament. In 1649 and again on 27 March 1660, an indenture records that Thomas Gill and Richard Willcoxson purchased from Ralph and Ellen a messuage and tenement called North Hill which included the fields mentioned before. In consideration they were to pay £110 to Ralph, £8 a year to Philip and £200 within two years of Philip's death to whoever then held the lands. Previously, on 27 October 1634, this property was conveyed by Philip Bostock to William Oldfield of Leftwich and Thomas Minshull of Bradwell as trustees for the use of Philip, his wife Frances and their issue; at this time mention was made of a cottage occupied by Laurence Oakes.[17]

Ralph appears in taxation returns of 1660 and 1664.[18] Described in the Poll Tax as 'Raph Bostocke gent', he had an income of £10 a year and paid four shillings tax for his property in Moulton and 3s 7d tax on property in Wharton worth £9 a year; he was also the collector of taxes for Moulton. Four years later he paid hearth tax on three hearths in his house. The family also appear in records concerning Northwich and at this time they held two salt houses in Northwich; one in Seath Street facing the Market Place, which was later owned by the Pickmere of Hulse, and the other in Yate Street. On 14 October 1662, Ralph presented Thomas Johnson, cobbler, of Over to the Quarter Sessions for poaching – night walking, cutting fish reels and destroying fish.[19] Ralph lived to be eighty years of age and outlived his eldest son and some of his relations: he was buried at Davenham on 30 January 1683. By his will dated 1699, a Nathaniel Bostock of Leftwich left 'all ye rest and residue of all my mortal goodes' to Ralph Bostock of Moulton, his kinsman.

Philip Bostock of Moulton was born in 1636 and married Margaret Chawley at Davenham on 4 June 1659. According to the Poll Tax returns Philip had an income of £20 a year and paid four shillings tax and lived with his three spinster daughters – Elizabeth, Ellen and Marie – who together paid three shillings tax.20 Philip does not appear in the Hearth Tax returns and may have been living with his father in the family home.

On 19 December 1680, he made his will. In it he mentions his daughters Mary, Martha, Ellen, Elizabeth and Eleanor who were to be paid £100 each within two years of his death by their brothers Philip and Ralph. Philip's wife Margaret was to hold messuages and tenements in 'Preston on ye Hill' and in Astley near Legh, Lancashire, until their son Ralph became of age, keeping him 'in meat and drink lodging and apparel' and ensuring that his name was added to the new lease. The major part of the estate, which included property in Wharton and Northwich, was left to the son and heir Philip who could only enter his patrimony on the death of Ralph Bostock, 'the elder'. The estate included lands and messuages in Moulton Moss held by Thomas Leicester, carpenter, Ralph Ravenscroft, webster, and William Barnshaw; in Wharton, held by George Wetherall of Guilden Sutton, a silkster, and in Northwich by George Robinson, shoemaker. Philip had two other sons, Thomas and William, who both moved to live in Knutsford and whose wills are dated 1722 and 1726 respectively. Thomas states he was the son of Philip and had issue by his wife Abigail – Thomas, John and Mary – and had property in Wales, Staffordshire, Shropshire and the city of Chester. William mentions his sons George and William and daughters Elizabeth Radcliffe of Marple and Mary Yarwood of Knutsford. The inventory of Philip's goods amounted to £283 16s 9d. Philip, junior, was born circa 1665 and married Mary daughter of Thomas Weston of Christleton, clerk, in 1686. The couple had four children: Peter (baptised in 1690), Ralph who died in infancy, Christine who also died young, and Frances.

MIDDLEWICH

For many centuries the name of Bostock is associated with the salt industry and the town of Middlewich. During the early medieval period there are occasional references to Bostocks of Middlewich but it is not certain whether there was ever a distinct branch at that time. Much of what follows comes from the *Middlewich Chartulary* a series of charters collected together in the seventeenth century by the antiquarian William Vernon.[20]

In the fifteenth century a family did settle here and their genealogy up to 1498 is detailed in a manuscript among the Harleian papers which has already been referred to in previous chapters.[21] It refers to Henry Bostock, younger brother to Sir Ralph Bostock (1392-1419) and son of Adam III Bostock. This Henry seems to be the same man that served in France, at Gisors, Normandy, under Edmund Beaufort, later duke of Somerset. Henry Bostock, who settled at Huxley, married Alison, daughter of Thomas Brett of Davenham, and had eight sons and three daughters: William, Thomas, Richard, Ralph, John, Hamnet, Edward, Roger, Maud, Margaret and Elizabeth. The eldest son William married Margery, daughter and heiress of Thomas Mason of Middlewich, and had nine sons and five daughters: Robert, Charles, Richard, Arthur, John, Humphrey, John, Ralph, James, Ellen, Margaret, Alice, Elizabeth, and Margery. The couples' marriage contract dated 1450/1 stipulated that Thomas Mason was to invest them with the perpetual rights to all his lands in Middlewich (both Adam IV Bostock and an Adam son of David Bostock witnessed the deed. On 28 September 1495, the following, who seem to be William's children, are recorded as holding salt-houses in the town according to the *Middlewich Chartulary*: Charles had three houses; William held four; Richard had two; Robert had two; and Margaret had one. Arthur Bostock of Middlewich had a lease of a salt house in Halphpenny Hill, about 1509, and he seems to have been the same person who occurs in documents in 1537 and again between 1544 and 1580 when there are records of him paying taxes on two salt houses.

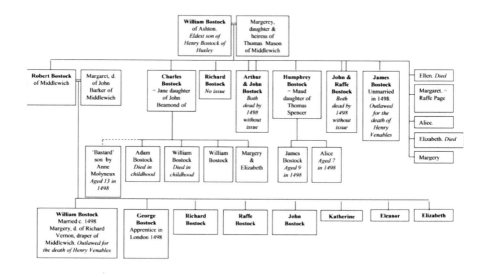

The Bostocks of Middlewich.
(Based on Harl. MS. 2059)

William and Margaret's eldest son was Robert who also appears in few documents relating to property in the town. He married Margaret, daughter of John Barker of Middlewich and had five sons and three daughters: William, George, Richard, Raffe, John, Katherine, Eleanor, and Elizabeth. In 1480/81, William, son of Sir Edward Holt of Wimboldsley, granted to Robert a plot of land in Newton at a rent of eight shillings a year. The land was described as being between the land of Robert Worrell on the east side and the king's road on the west and in length between the land of John Smith and the highway. On 16 November 1502, Jane Holt granted Robert and Margaret Bostock two closes in 'Reddysh' to hold for their lifetimes at a rent of 20s a year.

But the Bostocks of Middlewich are far from being straightforward. Robert Bostock heads the family tree of three generations in Laurence Bostock's papers. This starts by saying 'To this Robert his father gave lands in the Middlewich and others thereto adjoining the which called Bostocks of the Middlewich to this day 1576' and that Robert was descended of a third son of the lords of Bostock. It has a heading which reads 'Bostock of ye Orrell in Middlewich', but this location eludes me: I know Middlewich well but have never heard of 'Orrell', which means 'ore hill', and place-name references fail to mention it or any similar sounding name. The eldest son and heir is shown as being William who lived in Down Hatherley, near Gloucester, who married Tomasin, daughter of Robert Bostock of Moreton Say, Shropshire, and had

88

two daughters,one of whom married a Molton and settled in Churchdown, Gloucester, and the other married and lived in Northamptonshire. The second son is shown as John who married Margery daughter of Mathew Swettenham and had a son Ralph, who married Eleanor Beckett and had two daughters by her, and a daughter Eleanor who married Roger Page. The third son, Ralph, married a daughter of Leigh of Chester and had sons Henry and Ralph. Finally, Robert daughter was Katherine who married a member of the Blackbourne family.[22] Another version, which from other evidential sources is likely to be incorrect, contains much the same information but places John as son of Robert and father of William.[23]

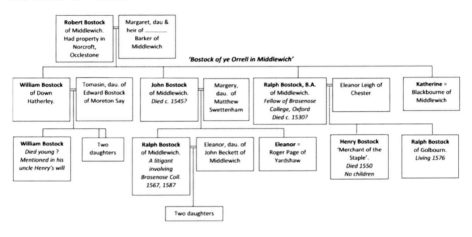

The Bostocks of Middlewich.
(Based on Harl. MS. 245 and papers relating to the Brasenose College Case)

William, Robert's eldest son, married Margery, daughter of Richard Vernon of Middlewich, who was a 'draper'. As the 1498 genealogy states 'But they have not leene together' it seems that they were either newly married or about to marry. This William and his uncle James were outlawed at the shire court held in Chester at Michaelmas 1498 for the murder of Henry Venables, son of William Venables. In the court rolls for 23 August 1496, there is mention of Henry Venables and George Spenser being fined for assaulting James (Jacob) Bostock in Kinderton Street, whilst he was fined for carrying a bill. These incidents were presumably part of a long-standing feud with the Venables family that had originally broken out in the 1470s between Ralph II, lord Bostock, and the Venables family over inheritance to the barony of Kinderton. I have so far not been able to trace the outcome of the indictments against

William and James for murder. George Bostock, Robert's second son, was in late 1498 bound as an apprentice in London.

In 1517/18, Robert entrusted William, his son and heir, Humphrey Penketham, Ralph Bostock, B.A., and the vicar of Middlewich with a messuage and lands in Occlestone called 'Norcroft' and other premises in Middlewich for the use of himself and his heirs. Six years later he entrusted Ralph Bostock, B.A., Ralf Vernon, cleric, Richard Davenport, John Folville and William Venables with lands and salt-houses in Middlewich and Newton to the use of himself and his wife Margaret for their lives and their sons. In January 1532, a Robert Bostock of Middlewich granted lands there called 'Bancroft' or 'Bromecroft' to Brasenose College, Oxford. A few years later, William Bostock of Down Hatherley, Gloucestershire, granted to Mathew Smyth, principal of the King's Hall, Oxford, and its scholars, eight messuages, two salt-houses, eight gardens, four acres of land, two of meadow and four of pasture in Middlewich and Newton. This was followed by a final agreement between the parties dated 6 August 1538, though by this time the properties were described as seven messuages, two acres of land, a barn and two cottages. This grant was subject to a long-running dispute with the college in 1587 from which it is apparent that Robert was a son of William Bostock of Asheton and Margaret Barker. This couple's other children were Henry; William of Downe Hatherley; Ralph, fellow of Brasenose College and senior bursar there in 1526,who died in about 1530; John who died *circa* 1545 leaving a son Ralph; and three daughters, Katherine, Eleanor and Isabel. In 1549, William's son Henry Bostock, a merchant of the Staple (a wool merchant), built a wool house on Brasenose College land in Steeple Aston, Oxfordshire, in return for a 20 years rent free lease of it: he seems not to have made use of it as the wool-house was usually leased to the rector.[24] That he was a Middlewich man is clear from his will dated 20 April 1549 (proved 7 November 1551) in which he mentions his next-of-kin in Middlewich 'of his name' and left money for the poor of Middlewich. The will also mentions William Bostock of Down Hatherley and his son William (who is not mentioned in the Harleian pedigrees), then under twenty-one; his servant Robert Bostock; Ralph Bostock, who was under twenty-one and 'now in the Mase with the glaziers' (a reference to him being a student at Brasenose College); Joan Coope who was 'lyke to be my wief'; his mistress Margaret Kyrton; and his nephews of the Blackbourne family.

Other references from the *Middlewich Chartulary* are as follows. In 1550 an Edward Bostock held a 'deeming house' and Robert had two of the same and on 24 October 1558, the 'widow' Bostock is also known to have held two 'deeming houses'. On 12 March 1567, Osmund de Vernon of Wells granted to Robert Bostock a messuage and cottage with a garden that lay in Pepper Street, Middlewich in consideration of a payment of £13 6s 8d. An Edward Bostock of Middlewich paid 6d for a parcel of ground at the end of his dwelling house in Wheelock Street, and William Bostock paid 2s 8d rent for a house there, and Ralph Bostock paid chief rent of two shillings for Brazenose College. John Bostock had a barn in Middlewich for which he paid 3s 4d rent. Finally, on 8 September 1590 Ralph Bostock of Middlewich sold to Thomas Egerton, then the Queen's Solicitor General, for 200 marks, all his messuages, lands and rents in Middlewich and Newton, except for two salt houses.

Charles Bostock of Middlewich left a will, dated 1611, which mentions his brother Ralph, who had issue Charles, John and Ralph; a sister Katherine, a John Bostock, a sister-in-law Ann Bostock a cousin George Boomand, a Hugh Berkett (Beckett) of Sutton, and his step mother Mrs. Bostock.

In the Middlewich church registers we find Bostocks occurring up from time to time, but not as often as one might expect given the many names that occur in other contemporary sources. The first two references are to Ottiwell, son of Robert Bostock who was christened on 3 August 1588, and Cicely, daughter of Thomas on 9 September the same year, but I suspect that these are in fact members of the Moulton branch. There are then no entries until 1600 and a spattering thereafter. Members of the Bostocks of Middlewich also occur in the registers at Church Minshull and Little Budworth: at the latter place as Ottiwell Bostock married a Margery Pownall in September 1610. Fitting these people into a genealogy is difficult.

In the Poll Tax of 1660 we find an Alice Bostock of Middlewich, widow; at Wimboldsley we have Ottiwell Bostock a husbandman earning £12 10s 0d a year living with Marie Bostock, widow, who had an annual income of £8 10s 0d. In the Hearth Tax of 1664 we find in Middlewich, Thomas Bostock and John Bostock each assessed at one hearth at Wimboldsley, three Marys, a Nicholas and an Eleanor each assessed at one hearth, and at Occlestone, a Thomas also assessed at one hearth.[25]

Returning to the Henry Bostock who died in 1551 it is interesting to note that he was a wool merchant as were the Bostocks of Abingdon, Berkshire, but it posses a question about links with one of the Bostocks of Churton who married a girl from the village of Steeple Barton, two miles away from Steeple Aston where Henry had a wool-houses - perhaps these distant relations kept in touch with one another.

LEFTWICH

During the seventeenth century a Bostock family lived in Leftwich. According to Burke's *Landed Gentry*, William, the head of this branch of the family, was the second son of Edward Bostock of Bostock (c.1550-1600). William we know was baptised at Davenham on 20 October 1586, married Ellen on 16 July 1603 and had a number of children: Joan, baptised on 29 September 1612; Margery on 26 December 1613; Catherine on 18 May 1615; Ellen on 20 September 1616; Margaret baptised on 16 March 1618; Cheney baptised on 3 February 1621; Elizabeth baptised on 4 November 1624; Isabel baptised on 31 July 1628; Mary baptised on 25 March 1630; and William baptised on 20 October 1633. The use of the name Cheney as a first name is interesting and clearly relates to William's mother, Margery Cheney.

A will, dated 15 July 1659, gives some insight into William's family and friends. William styles himself 'yeoman' and was probably fairly well off from farming his own lands, with an income of around £40 a year. Shortly before his death he conveyed his estate to his two friends, William Leftwich and John Blease, to be held by them for specified purposes and he willed that the conveyance and assignment 'stand true and irrevocable'. To Cheney, his eldest son, he gave a great bedstead, which stood in the 'chamber over the parlour' and that had once belonged to his uncle Henry. Cheney also received his father's tables, boards, forms and benches that were within the house and buildings; also two Bibles, a warming pan, a malt mill, the furnace, the 'great brandrett' (a metal gridiron for supporting cooking vessels over an open hearth), half of all the carts and ploughs and other implements of husbandry. The rest of William's goods, chattels and cattle were to be valued and sold, and out of the money raised Eleanor and Margery, his two eldest daughters, were to receive £40 each and the younger daughter Elizabeth, £20. Any remainder, plus debts owing to him, were to be divided up amongst all his children, except for Cheney. He named William Leftwich, son of William Leftwich of Northwich, John Blease of Leftwich, and his son Cheney as executors. William Hewit and William Leftwich senior witnessed the will. It was signed simply 'Wm B'.

Cheney Bostock was a soldier in his youth and early manhood and rose to the rank of captain. According to the pedigree in *Landed Gentry* he was the captain of the guard in charge of the scaffold at the execution of King Charles I in 1649. He is known to have served in the regiment commanded by Colonel Brooke and was one of five captains with responsibility for several hundred men who had been recruited in the hundreds of Northwich, Eddisbury and Bucklow. The same pedigree states that he was the last of the family to reside at Bostock Hall – but there are serious doubts about this and certainly no evidence. At the time the Hall was occupied by members of the Mainwaring family and Cheney's branch of the family had earlier lived at North Hill House in Bostock. Added to this, his father lived in Leftwich and for a time, in the 1650s, Cheney lived in Chester before moving back to Davenham parish. Cheney's name occurs in the tax returns of 1660 and 1664 as living in Leftwich. In the Poll Tax returns for 1660 his income was recorded as £30 a year, on which he paid tax of £1, and he was described as a husbandman with three servants - George Moores, Ann Parker and. Elizabeth Cornhill. In the Hearth Tax returns for 1664, he paid tax on three hearths indicating that he lived in a fairly large house. From the 1670s Cheney resided on a tenement in Leftwich.

In January 1689, Cheney is mentioned in documents recording a dispute to the right to a pew in Davenham church. The right centred around the ownership of lands known as 'Clayton's Tenement' a parcel of lands associated with Old Brett Hall in Leftwich. Sixty-nine years old John Leftwich stated that he remembered that the previous owner of Old Brett Hall, Mr Wych (William Wych of Alderley) selling the property to Cheney Bostock following the death of his tenant Robert Clayton, and that by 1688 the property had passed to Cheney's son William. Other witnesses testified that the tenement was associated with a particular seat in the church and reference was made to a plan of the church made in 1635. Those who opposed Cheney's right to what had been Mr Wych's seat said that Cheney had another seat for when he attended church 'which is not often he being a Dissenter'.' On the church plan the seat in question can be seen marked 'Richard Wych Cl..' referring to the Wych families 'Clayton's tenement'.

Cheney married a woman called Mary, and by her had a number of children some of whom were baptised at Davenham: Mary, on 29 April 1661; George, 7 January 1663; Eleanor, 27 March 1666. In the registers of Holy Trinity, Chester, are the following: Mary, baptised on 5 June 1657 and buried in November 1658 in the middle chancel; John, baptised on 28 January 1660, and another Mary, baptised on 10 February 1661. In the Chester registers Cheney is described as either 'esquire' or 'gentleman', but in Davenham he is simply 'yeoman' or 'householder'. The son George died in infancy and was buried on 11 January 1662.

Cheney made his will on 12 May 1675, when aged 55 years. Like his father before him, he asked to be buried at Davenham, either in the church or the churchyard. He mentions his lands, tenements and hereditaments in Leftwich, Davenham and elsewhere in the county, of which he was 'seized in fee simple' (held absolutely). His whole estate, real and personal, his lands, messuages, houses and tenements, together with their appurtenances, were to be granted to his eldest son William, and his male heirs. William was required to then pay to Cheney, the second son, the sum of £500 within three years of their father's death. A similar sum was to be paid to John, the third son, within six years. Presumably the moneys going to the younger sons when they reached the age of 21 years. The will clearly states that the estate was to be inherited by male heirs only, and that if William had no sons then Cheney was to inherit and so on. If William, Cheney and John died without lawful heirs, then William Bostock of Nantwich, 'gentleman', Cheney's brother, was to inherit the estate. He would then pay the sisters, Margery (whose husband's name cannot be deciphered); Ellen Sproston, widow; Elizabeth wife of Humphrey Pownall; and Isabel wife of Robert Wrench, certain sums of money. All remaining goods, chattels and cattles were granted to William, the eldest son, who along with Ralph Cheney, blacksmith, of Northwich, were named as executors. Brother William, John Simcock of Ridley, and Robert Wrench of Moulton, yeoman, were named as feoffees (trustees). An addition to the will allowed the sum of £20 to be paid to Cheney's wife Mary as an annual pension, and instructed that the third son John was to receive the sum of £8 a year for two years after Cheney's death, with a final payment of £30. The witnesses were John Pownall, Peter Fletcher, Elizabeth Touchet and William Leftwich. The will is sealed with the Bostock shield of arms, differenced by a crescent to indicate decent from a second son. Cheney was buried at Davenham on 18 May 1675; his widow Mary was buried on 5 June in the same year. In Burke's *Landed Gentry*, Cheney's brother William is said to have married an Abigail Swettenham who died in 1683; he dying on 31 December 1687.

The baptisms of William, Cheney and John do not appear in local parish registers, however the will seems to hold a clue as to their ages. As feoffees were appointed, William was probably under 21 years of age, say nineteen or twenty, Cheney was probably eighteen and due to receive a sum of money in three years time, and John was fifteen and due to receive his share in six years. John's estimated age fits with the entry in the registers of Holy Trinity church mentioned above which also show his birth date as 6 January. In the same church, on 24 April 1691, John married Mary, daughter of Samuel Smallwood of Chelford, by whom he had issue and descendants who lived in a number of places before finally settling in Kent.

The pedigree in *Landed Gentry* suggests that William and Cheney, the two elder boys died without issue and that John Bostock, the third son, inherited the estates. I have not found any evidence from which to draw that conclusion. In fact, William, the eldest son is probably identical with the William Bostock who on 18 October 1680, married Ellen Moore at Davenham. The couple had a son, Philip, baptised on 11 July 1686. Another William Bostock, described as 'gentleman' of Leftwich died in 1697, and as he did not leave a will, administration of his estate was granted to his widow Susanna.

REFERENCES AND NOTES FOR CHAPTER FIVE

Much of what relates to Middlewich comes from deeds in the Middlewich Chartulary. A 'burgesship' is a right to trade in salt and do business in a town. A 'deeming house' is a type of salt-house which paid a particular form of rent. The wills referred to are all to be found in the wills collection of Cheshire Archives and Local Studies.

The case concerning Bostock Family *v.* Brasenose College is discussed at length in *Middlewich Chartulary*, vol II, pp. xiii - xxiii. See also Bostock A.J., 'Cheshire's Seat of Learning: Brasenose College, Oxford', *Cheshire History*, vol. 56 (2016)

1. Domesday Book, f. 265a
2. Ormerod, III, p 264
3. Harleian Society, vol. xviii, pp 27, 29
4. Harl. MS 245 f.161v. Merton, or Marton, and Bradford are areas on the opposite side of the River Weaver that became parts of the Vale Royal Abbey estates.
5. Harl. MS 2077; Harl. MS 245 f.161v.
6. Harl. MS 139 f.100 & 245 f.161v.
7. The manuscript in Harl. MS 245 has her as sole heir of 'Thomas Sooton of Wicksall' alongside which is noted 'I think Salt of Yoxall'
8. Harl. MS 139 f.100
9. *Cheshire Sheaf*, September 1920, p 88.
10. Some say Jane 'Galley of Swaneylone'(Swanlow Lane).
11. Harleian Society, vol. xviii, p. 30
12. *Calendar of Patent Rolls 1572-1575*, p 245 (C66/1112)
13. *op cit*, 1575-1578, p 329 (C66/1158)

14. Middlewich Chartulary, p 357
15. CRO: DVE1/MIX/4
16. Cheshire Quarter Sessions
17. CRO: DFN 2705/2
18. Lawton, G. O.(ed.), 'Northwich Hundred: Poll Tax 1660 and Hearth Tax 1664', *Record Society of Lancashire and Cheshire*, vol. cxix (1979) pp. 154, 242
19. Quarter Sessions records
20. Varley, J (ed.), A Middlewich Chartulary, *Chetham Society*, 2 volumes, (1941,1944)
21. Harl. MS. 2059
22. Harl MS 245
23. Harl. MS 139 f.103
24. Baggs,A.P., *et al*, 'Parishes: Steeple Aston', in *A History of the County of Oxford:* Volume 11, Wootton Hundred (Northern Part), ed. Alan Crossley (London, 1983), pp. 21-44
25. Lawton, op cit.

7.   THE BOSTOCKS OF ELSEWHERE IN CHESHIRE

There were dozens of branches of the family who settled within Cheshire from which many people today with the Bostock surname will be descended. It would be far too tedious to mention them all as, invariably, only basic family details are known. Branches may be traced to Chester, Cuddington, Huntington, Malpas, Somerford, Swettenham, Sandbach, Warmingham, Coppenhall, Nantwich and elsewhere as indicated on the map. Below are some of the more important families about whom some details are available.

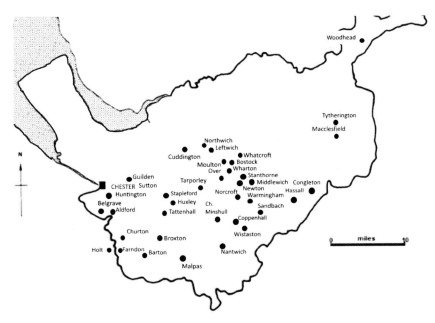

Some of the places in which Bostock Families settled in Cheshire

BARTON AND BELGRAVE

This branch of the family is a part of the Churton branch (*see below*) descending from John, second son of Robert Bostock and Alice Snelston of Churton. The family tree appears in two parts of the Harleian Collection. John Bostock settled at Barton and married Joyce daughter and heir of William Bulkeley of Broxton. The herald William Smith in his large pedigree of the Bostock family records John Bostock of Barton as a son of Sir Adam Bostock but corrects himself by use of a symbol to make him son of the Churton branch, however another document in the Harleian collection repeats this mistake.[1]

There were four successive generations of John. The second John married Joyce Golbourn of Golbourn Bellew; the next married Margaret Willaston of Willaston, Whitchurch, and the fourth married Katherine Heath of Clutton. This last John had sons Richard and Hugh, and daughters Margaret, who married Raffe David of Whitchurch, and Katherine, who married Ralph Huxley of Sidnall. In 1543, John Bostock of Barton and a John Barker, clerk, recovered three messuages and fifty-two acres of land (including an acre of wood and marsh) in Tilston and elsewhere from a William Ayre.

The family resided here for many more generations as a Richard Bostock of Broxton was a freeholder here in 1580 and a John of Barton left a will in 1730 which mentions his wife Barbara and children John, Joseph, Mary and Ann.

John Bostock and Joyce Bulkeley's second son was named Richard. He married and had a son named John. This John married a Anne Hanky who inherited property in Belgrave and hence the branch that settled there. They had two sons: John who married Elizabeth Evans from Hawarden, and had two sons and three daughters; and a second son Hugh.

The last John's eldest son, George Bostock of Belgrave, yeoman, left a will in 1610 which sates that his wife was to 'have and enjoy the moiety of my tenement in Belgrave during her widowhood'. It mentions children, Katherine, Anne and Thomas who were all under twenty-one years of age and were to receive the residue of his goods; his son and heir was also named George. Cousins John Dicus and John Edwards are mentioned as is a bequest to the repair of Eccleston church. His inventory of goods totals £173 2s 0d. George's widow, Mary, remarried William Whittle.

CHURTON

Churton is a township that lies alongside the river Dee, six miles south of Chester, and the family that settled here is one of the important branches. When William Webb visited the area he wrote that here 'is situate two gentlemen's habitations of the Barnstons and the Bostocks'. Details of the family's descent are recorded in the *Visitation of Cheshire 1580* and in a few other Harleian manuscripts in the British Library.[2]

The family starts with David Bostock who was a younger son of Adam III Bostock, lord of Bostock (c.1330 – 1374) and probably born circa 1370. One of the pedigree in the Harleian collections begins with the statement 'In ye tyme of Sir John de Ardern Lord of Audford, David de Bostok, 2 or 3 sonne to ye Lord of Bostok, came to Churton in ye parish of Farndon, ... The said David married Margaret d. of one Dee (a kinswoman to ye said L. of Audford with whom ye said L. of Audford gave certain landes &tc. and they had issue'.[3] From the paragraph just quoted it is clear that David came by his estate in Churton by marriage. David occurs in 1395 as surety for his brother Adam, in the sum of £200, to keep the peace towards the abbot of Vale Royal and then, three years later, he occurs as an archer in the bodyguard of King Richard II and journeyed to Ireland in that capacity. In July 1400, he went to Scotland as a man-at-arms under the captaincy of Sir John Eton.

Robert, son of Robert, son of David, married Alice daughter and heir of Robert Snelston, esquire, and heir of her mother, Margery who was a co-heir to Thomas Shocklach and inherited half that manor: through this valuable marriage Robert will have acquired further lands. He occurs in 1434, when aged about 40, in a lease of lands in Overmarsh for himself and Brian de Barnston. Robert had two sons: Robert who continued at Churton and John who settled at nearby Barton (*see above*).

The next Robert (the third so named) occurs in 1489 as a surety in a recognizance. He married his cousin Jane, an illegitimate daughter of the last Adam lord of Bostock, by whom he had a son, Robert. This Adam apparently bought the other half share of lands in Shocklach. He married for a second time to Dorothy, daughter of Sir George Calveley of Lea, by whom he had a son named Lancelot, one of Queen Elizabeth I's Gentleman Pensioners: Lancelot's family settled at Holt, Denbighshire(*see later account*). After her husband's death, Dorothy married an Edward Almer and had another son. In 1492 Robert gave evidence at an enquiry into the age of a Richard Clive of Huxley and stated that he was fifty years old.

Robert IV occurs with his father in the recognizance of 1489 and also occurs in 1490 and in 1504 as a collector of subsidies for the Broxton Hundred. He married Margaret, daughter of Richard Norris of Speke, esquire. Robert had a sister named Alice who was the wife of a Peter Wells who lived in Yorkshire. He also had a brother named Charles who never married but had an illegitimate son, by Helen Tayboner, named Robert who became an army captain serving in Ireland with 'great estimation', though I have found no record of him in State Papers. Although the captain married an Anne Tilston he had no children by her but, instead, fathered an illegitimate son and daughter whose names are not recorded.

John Bostock of Churton seems to be the head of the next generation and he occurs in 1450 and was later listed as a freeholder who was able to supply four men for military service. He married Matilda daughter of Hugh Holme of Coddington. On the day of his death John held twenty messuages, one thousand acres of land, one hundred acres of pasture, twenty of woodland, one hundred of meadow, ten of heathland, twenty of moor land and meadow, and ten acres of water. These properties lay in the townships of Churton, Farndon, Shocklach, Calcott, Chester, Dodleston, Pulford, Calveley and Grafton. His estate suffered a recovery of some lands by Richard Grosvenor, Ralph Bostock of Aldford, David Dodd of Edge and John Heth.

At one time in Farndon church there was memorial widow to the memory of John Bostock which showed the family coat of arms of the Bostocks of Churton and of Barton and the words 'Orate pro bono statu Johis Bostock et Matild' uxoris eius qui hanc opus vitria'. [4] Another version gives much the same with the date 1531 and has drawings of the coats of arms but says they were in the church of 'Snelston by ye Holt'.[5]

John had four sons and six daughters and as his eldest son Robert predeceased him his grandson George became heir to the Churton estate and is listed as a freeholder here in 1580. He married Ann, daughter and co-heir of John Hanky of Churton and died in 1620 and was buried in the chancel of Farndon church on 30 November: his will was proved the following year. Besides several daughters he had the following sons: John who died young, George, Edward, Richard and Robert. A pulpit cloth once contained the coat of arms of Bostock impaling Hanky with the inscription 'ex dono G.B. et Anne ux'. George's wife Ann left a will dated 17 January 1622 (proved on 8 April 1622) which mentions their sons Robert, Richard and George and daughters Alice (Harpur), Jane (Irishe), Elizabeth (Fletcher), Dorothy and Mary.

At the time of his father's death George junior was aged 27. He occurs in 1619 with Edward Bostock of Aldford on a summons to the Quarter Sessions for not scouring their ditches in Aldford that lay along the highway from Chester to Edgerley and Coddington. Four years later he and his cousin George Bostock of Holt, occur in a document that records the descent of Captain William Bostock of Woodhead (*see later section*). He had two marriages: first, Alice, daughter of John Croker of Steeple Barton, Oxfordshire, and second, Katherine, daughter of Katherine Whitmore of Thurstaston. This second wife's funeral certificate records that she died on 8 May 1632 and was buried at Aldford church. His daughter Frances married Robert Draper, merchant, of London, 1634.

George's *inquisition post mortem* was heard at Northwich on 18 January 1639. It records that his son and heir was George and that he had another son named Robert. Mention is also made of Lancelot Bostock of Aldford who was probably a cousin and perhaps son of the Robert Bostock who held property there in 1618. The Edward Bostock of Aldford mentioned above left a will in 1624 which mentions his son and heir Robert Bostock of London.

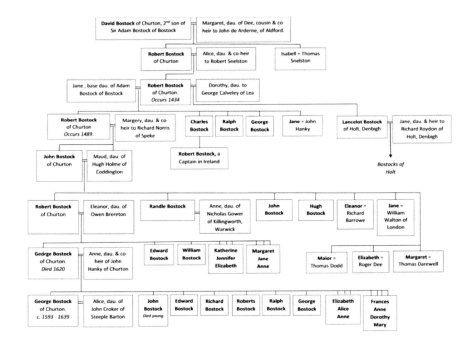

The Bostocks of Churton .
(Based on Harl. MS. 139, 245, 1424, 1505.)

CONGLETON

John Bostock, born circa 1640, son of John Bostock of Macclesfield, son of William of Wildboarclough, resided at Broken Cross, Macclesfield. His son and heir, John, moved to Congleton.

On 9 February 1696, John Bostock of Macclefield married Elizabeth Smith of Congleton at Gawsworth church. Before the couple settled in Congleton they had a number of children baptised at Macclesfield: Elizabeth (1699), Maria (1701), John (1704), Esther (1707), Sarah (1709), Charles (1710) and Ethena (1712). At some time prior to 1718 the family moved to Congleton where James and another John were baptised in 1718 and 1720 respectively. Of these children Charles became a schoolmaster in Macclesfield and, on 4 November 1728, was admitted to St Johns College, Cambridge, died three years later and was buried in Congleton. The younger son James also died young and was buried on 19 July 1722. In the 1720s John became an Alderman of the Borough of Congleton and was elected mayor in 1726, 1732, 1738 and 1747. He was buried at Congleton on 9 December 1755.

The surviving son John, born in 1720, married twice: first to Ann Shaw of Congleton in October 1741; secondly, at Astbury church, Elizabeth Brown on 4 July 1759. By his first marriage he had a daughter Sarah in 1742, and by his second marriage: John (who died aged 6 years), Jane, Francis, William and another John who died aged 2 years). John Bostock, gentleman, of Congleton left a will dated 1767 which was proved in 1771. He left money to his sister Elizabeth and daughter Sarah, and the estates in Gawsworth and Macclesfield he left to his son Francis; a nephew, Joseph Bednall of Leek is also mentioned. John was buried at Congleton on 27 June 1769.

Francis Bostock was educated at Manchester Grammar School. He became a surgeon with a practice in Newcastle under Lyne. He married Sarah Robinson in 1800 and had a number of children. On retiring to his estates in Congleton he made his will in February 1820 and was buried in March that year. His will recites that he held 'messuages, lands, tenements, hereditaments and real estate' at Broken Cross, Long Moss, Whirley and Congleton. These properties were left to trustees for the benefit of his daughters Elizabeth and Sarah: he also mentions his sister Jane Bostock. William, the second son, was similarly educated and became a surgeon in Longton, near Newcastle. He married Priscilla Adney and had children: Priscilla Aubin, born in 1794 (died unmarried in 1853) and John Adney who lived in Congleton. The family are commemorated by a plaque in St Peter's church.

During the 1740s there was another Bostock family in Congleton. John Bostock, a chandler, and Mary Wright were married there in 1753: previously John had a wife called Ann but she died in 1753. He may be John son of John of Macclesfield. Later in the 1760s there is mention of a John Bostock, an innkeeper, and his wife Mary.

COPPENHALL

The father of Laurence Bostock, the antiquary, had a house here, but exactly where and how those who continued to reside here were related to him his not known. The branch settled in Coppenhall seem to have had links with neighbouring families at Haslington and Warmingham. Without going into any detail of those families it is worth mentioning a particular character – Bridget Bostock.

Bridget Bostock was a faith healer who is colloquially known as 'the White Witch of Coppenhall'.[6] What is particularly interesting is that such an obscure woman from Cheshire should become so famous. She first appears as the subject of two letters to the Gentleman's Magazine of September 1748; the first of these reads:

> *'Middlewych in Cheshire, Aug.28. There is risen up in the country a great doctress, an old woman, who is resorted to by all ranks and degrees; to be cured of all diseases; she lives four miles from hence, and has been in great fame about two months; she has several hundred of patients in a day out of all the country round for 30 miles: I went to see her yesterday out of curiosity, and believe near 600 people were with her I believe all the country are gone stark mad. The chief thing she cures with is fasting spittle' and 'God bless you with faith'.*

A letter written from 'Namptwich' and dated 28 August 1748, relates the wonderful cures done by Bridget and that she was the cause of as much talk as the Jacobite rebels were three years earlier. The correspondent also refers to the large numbers who attended the old woman's house saying that in twelve months the numbers had increased from forty to over a hundred. One Sunday, six hundred people were admitted to her presence, being allowed in five or six at a time: by six o'clock in the evening she still had sixty people waiting. The following Monday there were seven hundred, a number which became common. People travelled great distances to visit her. The writer remarks that whereas there was rarely a coach travelling along the lane, now there were three or four a day. Apparently, according to this same writer, Bridget would treat her patients before taking food and by means of stroking the afflicted with her saliva and praying for them. On many occasion she dealt with so many ill people that she grew faint with hunger as she would not eat until she had completed her days work. She cured blindness, deafness, lameness, rheumatism, 'the King's evil' or scoflila, hysteria, fits, shortness of breath, dropsy, palsy, leprosy, cancers - almost everything. She would not meddle with those suffering from the 'French disease' - syphilis. Her treatments were sometimes successful straightaway, for others they became well on their way home; few it is said failed to gain relief.

The curate of Coppenhall church, the Reverend William Harding, had a son cured of lameness by Bridget who was a regular worshipper at his church: doctors had previously failed him. A Mrs. Gradwell of Liverpool is said to have had her sight restored. During the summer of 1749 a Mr Christopher Lucas, a gardener of Thame, Oxfordshire, journeyed to visit Bridget with his wife who was suffering from palsy, as did a young lady who had been blind for five years and a grocer's wife with 'a pluresie in her side, incurable from the hospitals in and about London'. Bridget could not cure the first two but succeeded with the third. It was not just the working classes who flocked to her door or contacted her in the hope of some satisfaction. Sir John Pryce, of Newtown Hall, Montgomryshire, having heard about Bridget's miracles wrote to her in December 1748 and asked that she say prayers in an attempt to raise his third wife from the dead. He stated that he was prepared to send a coach and servants to fetch her and to pay all her expenses. It is said that Bridget did visit Sir John's house, but failed to bring Lady Eleanor Pryce back to life.

Whilst there were many who believed in her powers and travelled great distances to see her, Bridget had her critics too. Many were very sceptical and these included the Reverend George Reade, vicar of Over Peover. He doubted that anyone had been cured by her, 'nothing could happen to any of her patients, but what would certainly have happen'd, if they had stayed at home'. Though he also suggests that any benefit her patients may have gained would have been due to taking exercise by walking to see her. Another sceptic records 'she appears to me to be a very ignorant creature, ... the noise that this silly woman has made, even among the vulgar, is surprising; but that any person who pretends to any degree of sense, should be so deluded as to go near an hundred miles after her, is still more surprising.'

So who was this woman and what do we know of her? In September 1784, Bridget was housekeeper at 'old Bostock's house' in Coppenhall for which she received an annual income of thirty-five shillings. Her home was described as being four miles from Middlewich and three miles from both Sandbach and Nantwich, which would place her somewhere in the region of Maw Green, the northern part of Crewe, which itself was formed from the amalgamation of Church Coppenhall and neighbouring Monks Coppenhall. Certainly there were many branches of the Bostock family in the area as families may be found at neighbouring Warmingham, Minshull, Leighton, Wimboldsley and Haslington. To which branch she belonged is not clear as no reference can be found to any baptism or burial to any person of her name in the Cheshire parish registers - perhaps Bridget was not her given name. It is likely that whoever she was, she was a member of one of the families who resided at Coppenhall: the householders there being Acton, James and Richard each of whom were related to one another. A house in this area of Crewe is still known as Acton House which helps locate the area in which Bridget lived. The land tax returns for Church Coppenhall for 1787 refer to a house and land owned by James

Bostock and occupied by Richard Bostock, and 'late Bridget Bostock's, Doctres'. This holding was worth enough to pay 18s 8d. at the rate of four shillings in the pound and may be the 'great hall house' to which she had moved by August 1749. Both James and Acton left wills: 1786 and 1799 respectively. James was buried at Coppenhall on 28 October 1787.

In 1748, Bridget was described as being old, aged 64 according to one writer and 70 to another. When the Nantwich letter writer met her she was wearing a very plain dress, with a flannel waistcoat, a green linsey apron, a pair of clogs and a plain cap tied with 'halfpenny lace'. Another of her visitors described as an old shrivelled creature who was seated in an elbow chair, in a most dirty attire, and her petticoats not reaching half-way down her legs.

FARNDON

The Bostocks, and probably a junior line of the Churton branch, held lands in Farndon as early as the reign of King Henry VIII for at that time a John Bostock of Barton and a David Apova recovered from John Yerdsley three messuages and eighty acres in Churton and Farndon.

In 1636 a will was made by Thomas Bostock of Farndon which ordained that his house and lands in Crewe (by Farndon) and Farndon go to his son Edward. His other sons – Thomas, Richard and Ephriam – and daughters Mary (wife of Henry price of Saighton) and Katherine are also mentioned. Thomas' wife Jane Cotgreave, whom he married on 10 December 1610, received certain lands in Middlewich. The eldest son Edward seems to have become an ironmonger for in 1604 he was apprenticed to George Harpur, ironmonger, of Chester for eight years. In 1641 he married Ellen Minshull, a widow of St Peter's, Chester, but had no children by her. In his will dated 1645 he bequeathed his house and lands in Crewe and Farndon to his wife Ellen and thence, after her demise, to her daughter Mary Minshull. His son-in-law Francis Minshull is also mentioned as are his sisters Mary and Beaumande, a brother-in-law John Wrighte, and cousins Katherine Richardson, Robert Wilkinson, James Strongintharm, Richard Tucker, Richard Trafford and Edward Bostock. The last mentioned person held salt-houses in Middlewich.

It seems likely that a family of Bostocks who were ironmongers and lived in the parish of St Peter's in Chester were in some way related to Edward. In 1697 Jonathan Bostock is listed as an apprentice ironmonger with William Crue of Chester, and then two years later he married Mary Bridge on 1 September 1699 at St Mary's church, Chester, and the couple had five children. Throughout Jonathan is described as an ironmonger and his sons Richard and

Philip followed the same trade in the city and in Tarvin. A branch of this family is known to have moved to Liverpool and thence emigrated to Australia.

HASSALL

Originally this branch of the family lived at Bostock House, Hassall, in the parish of Sandbach: this was a fortified brick house surrounded by a moat. If the heraldry is correct then it seems that they were descended of a fourth son of the Bostocks of Bostock.

Among the Harleian Manuscripts in the British Library there is an account of this family written in the 1570s which starts with Humphrey Bostock of Sandbach, presumably meaning the parish.[8] The opening paragraph states that a younger brother of the 'chiefest house of Bostok' was known as 'Bostok of Sandbach'. This particular person married one of the heirs of the town of Little Hassall and from then on held the 'manor house called the hall of Bostok' paying 4d a year to the lord of Hassall. In all probability this first generation is represented by Hugh Bostock who, on 11 February 1434, with Adam Bostock, witnessed a settlement made by Abbot John de Wheathampstead (alias Bostock). His son was Humphrey Bostock who married Eleanor the sole heir of Robert Say of Moreton Say, Shropshire, and thus inherited property there. (*See Chapter 8*)

HUXLEY

This family descended from Henry, third son of sir Adam de Bostock of Bostock and Janet Bradshaw. Henry married Alice daughter of Thomas Brett of Davenham and after her death a daughter of Bostock of Moulton.

Henry had a number of children sons William, Thomas, Richard, Ralph, John, Hamnet, Edward, and Roger, and three daughters Maud, Margaret and Elizabeth. Of these, Roger died from a gun-shot wound at the Siege of 'Terwwyn' (this seems to refer to the campaign of Thérouanne and Tourney which culminated in the Battle of the Spurs in the summer of 1513). He didn't marry but had an illegitimate daughter named Jane. The eldest son William married Margery, daughter of Thomas Mason of Middlewich in 1451, which was witnessed by Adam Bostock of Bostock, Henry Bostock and Adam son of David Bostock. The majority of this family continued to reside in Middlewich (see previous chapter), though Thomas settled at Huxley. He married Jane widow of Thomas Hulgreave of Tilston, and was followed there by a son Hugh, whose children were all dead by 1498 according to the genealogy drawn up that year.

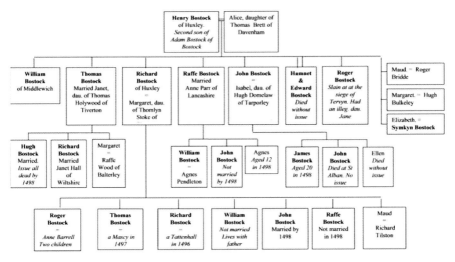

The Bostocks of Huxley.
(Based on Harl. MS 2059.)

Somehow, the family continued as a sixteenth century John Bostock of Huxley had two sons and two daughters. Hugh, married Ann, daughter of John Bruyn and widow of a Hockenhull, and an only daughter who married Henry Birkenhead; Ralph the second son married Ann daughter of Thomas Fisher by whom he had two only daughters: Katherine married a Tilston and Elizabeth who married George Manley of Huxley. Thus the main line of the Bostocks of Huxley came to an end in or about 1612.

Of Henry Bostock's other sons. Richard of Tattenhall married Margaret daughter of Thomas Stoke of Tiverton. Ralph married Agnes widow of Thomas Parr from Lancashire and John married Isabell Domelaw (*see Bostock of Tarporley*). Henry's daughters all married. Maude married a Roger Bridde; Margaret married Hugh Bulkeley of Broxton; and Elizabeth married a Symkyn Bostock, son and heir of Nicholas Bostock of Davenham, priest. This last couple had a son who died in childhood and so Symkyn's lands and tenements passed to his nephew Henry Bostock who was in possession in 1498. Nothing else is known of the Davenham branch.

MACCLESFIELD

The Bostocks of Macclesfield commence with Ralph Bostock of Wildboarclough, a place that lay in the extensive Macclesfield Forest. From him families settled in neighbouring Wincle, Harrop, Tytherington and Broken

Cross. Members of the family were prominent in the administration and affairs of the Borough of Macclesfield and held various offices in the Forest.

Ralph Bostock, gentleman, of Wildboarclough and his wife Emme had a child named Anne baptised at Macclesfield on 4 May 1599. The couple may have been the parents of Lancelot, who was baptised on 24 October 1588, and Isabel, who was baptised in February 1594. Ralph was buried on 25 January 1629 less than a year after his wife Emme who was buried on 10 May 1628.

In the Macclesfield registers from 1607 three distinct families are noticed: William Bostock of Wildboarclough, Hugh of Wildboarclough and Edward of 'ye chamber in ye forest'. There is no mention of a family of Lancelot, though on 4 April 1632 a man of that name married Margaret Brandreth, a daughter of John Brandreth, mayor of Macclefield in 1620/1. Interestingly Lancelot is a name found in the Churton and Holt branches, which might suggest a link.

Lancelot Bostock rose to a position of eminence within the area. In 1629 he became a churchwarden and had a grant of a seat in the church. Macclesfield was governed by its mayor, two aldermen, and twenty-four 'of the better and more honest burgesses' who acted as 'capital burgesses. Each year 'an honourable and discreet man' was elected to be the High Steward of the Borough and he with the mayor, past mayor, aldermen and capital; burgesses acted as justices of the peace for the borough. Lancelot became a capital burgess and an alderman.

On 16 December 1635, Dame Mary Savage of Bostock Hall was buried in Macclesfield along with her son Sir Thomas, Viscount Savage of Rock Savage. Nineteen years later, John Savage, the first earl Rivers, died in a fire at Frodsham castle and was brought to Macclesfield for burial. In that same year Lancelot was elected a mayor of the town: was that in respect for Savage, lord of the manor of Bostock? In October 1638 he was again elected mayor, in succession to Sir Edward Fitton of Gawsworth. Eight years later Lancelot held the office of Bailiff of the Forest, a title previously held by the Savage family, then represented by John, viscount Savage and earl Rivers. In 1661, Lancelot bought himself a seat on the front pew of the south aisle of the church for fifteen shillings. Four years later he bought another seat in the front of the 'new loft' on the south side, on a pew adjoining that of Earl Rivers; it cost him £1 10s 0d. His seating within the church certainly mark him as a person of some significance and social status.

In 1672, a Laurence Bostock, alderman, left a will. In it he mentions his possessions in Macclesfield Forest, his wife Ellen, brothers Edward and Hugh and Ellen Sumner, Hugh's late wife. He also mentions nephews and nieces:

Edward, Lancelot, Frances, Mary, Anne, Elizabeth and Susan, the children of Edward; and Charles, Thomas, Anne and Emme, the children of Hugh. It seems that Lancelot (or Laurence) died without issue at the age of 84.

Edward Bostock was born circa 1600 and lived at 'ye chamber in ye forest', a place was at the centre of forest administration and the lord's hunting lodge. Edward held the office of 'keeper of the forest' an authority subordinate to the bailiff and selected by him – at this time the Stanley family were the bailiffs. The keeper's duties were to supervise what was left of the forest and the chamber was the keeper's official residence. In 1626 Edward married Margaret, daughter of Henry Pott, whose brother Hugh some twenty years later took on the duties of 'keeper' and claimed 'ye chamber and ye ground thereto belonging'; he was eventually issued with a grant of the office by James lord Strange, in 1647. In the baptismal registers we find the following children of Edward and Margaret: Edward (November 1626), Lancelot (9 September 1629), Mary (23 February 1631), Ralph (25 March 1634 and died in infancy), Frances (26 October 1635) and Sarah (10 December 1638). At Sarah's christening Edward is described as 'de citeriori de Harrope' (of this side of Harrop) and was therefore no longer holding the office of keeper of the forest: Harrop was an area in which his wife's family lived. During the Civil War, Edward had Royalist sympathies and was listed in May 1648 as one of several persons who 'continue extremely malicious and very active against Parliament and should be remembered if further punishment be awarded to delinquents.

Hugh Bostock, born circa 1590, who was probably Edward's elder brother, had an illegitimate son named George baptised on 26 April 1613. After he married George's mother he had other children by her: Edmund (3 May 1616), Katherine (2 January 1619 and died in infancy) and Lancelot (12 July 1620). Anne Bostock died in 1627 and was buried on 28 September. Afterwards Hugh married an Ellen Sumner and had by her: Charles (24 July 1635), Samuel (3 March 1638), Thomas (13 March 1641 and died in infancy), Thomas (16 April 1645), Anne (22 November 1642), Emme (18 April 1647) and Edward (15 April 1649).

Lancelot, Edward and Hugh seem to belong to one generation and were probably sons of Ralph Bostock of Wildboarclough. But Ralph seems to have had a brother called William who also lived at Wildboarclough. He had a son named John baptised on 20 May 1607 and a daughter, Elizabeth, four years later. It is his line that we shall now follow.

John Bostock resided at Broken Cross, a hamlet on the west side of Macclesfield. He married Margery Bradbourne on 11 August 1634 and had at least six children some of whom appear in the registers. His will dated 1661 mentions the following: John (*see Bostocks of Congleton*), Francis, William, Elizabeth (married to John Whittaker), Sarah (married Joseph Orme on 19 June 1671) and Maria (wife of John Thorneycroft).

Francis Bostock lived in nearby Tytherington and is styled 'gentleman'. In 1684 he was elected as a 'capital burgess' of Macclesfield. Although there are no references in the registers to his marriage or any children, his will refers to sons David, Francis, William and John (who will each be referred to in the following paragraphs) and a daughter Elizabeth (Johnson). Francis' wife received the major part of the estate and the children the remainder with Francis receiving a tenement in Tytherington and property near Whirley (probably in Broken Cross) called 'Koos Wood'.

Of the second son William little is known beyond the fact that his inventory and letters of administration were drawn up in 1686. The younger son John became a chapman in Macclesfield and left a will in 1678. In it he mentions his son John who 'shall have the house I nowe live in with the buildings thereto belonging and the one half of my ground paying the rent I have been accustomed to pay for that part'. Next, he mentions his wife, Mary, who was to have the house in which her father lived, together with the outhouses and grounds. After her death he ordered that her share should go to John so that he might have all the messuages, tenements, houses, edifices, lands and premises at or near Broken Cross. To his brother William he gave twenty shillings and a like sum to his brothers-in-law John Whittaker, Joseph Orme and John Thorneycroft. The remainder of his goods were to be shared by his wife and children, including the child with whom his wife was then pregnant. The executors were his good friend Lawrence Downes of Tytherington and brother Francis; they were to manage the children's shares until they came of age. The will was proved on 9 October 1684.

Francis, John's eldest son lived in Tytherington and had a son David who like his uncle, was also a chapman. He was born about 1680 and according to a marriage bond of 1701 he appears to have married a Hannah Whittaker of Warmingham. Another bond dated 25 November 1709 names David and a Rebecca Clatham of Duckinfield. On 10 August 1709, David witnessed a marriage bond between Ralph Bostock of Clotton, near Tarvin) and Elizabeth Pinnington of Duddon: was Ralph a relation? David's children David (baptised on 8 July 1707) and Francis (24 June 1714) appear in the Macclesfield registers. Francis' second son was also called Francis and he to became a chapman. He married Anne Siddington, according to a bond of 24 June 1709, and had children: Francis, Ann and James. It may be the case that this Francis married earlier for on 14 March 1705 a Francis Bostock, of Park Lane, had a son Francis baptised. During his lifetime Francis was described as either 'of Macclesfield' or 'of Tytherington', and after 1711 as an alderman. The third son William may be identified with William Bostock of Waters Green, Macclesfield who had a son John and a daughter Josiah. The youngest son, John, is referred to in his father's will:

> ' I give and bequeath unto my son John all the household goods he hath of mine provided that he comes to account honestly with my executors and pays them what he is indebted to me, but if he refuses so to account and pay my executors shall take from him and give unto him twenty shillings'

In 1734, this John also left a will which mentions his children who were all less than 21 years old: John, Francis and David. The parish registers also show he had a number of other children who died young. John had the 'right and title' to the sixth pew in the middle rank of the north side of Macclesfield church, which he registered to himself and his heirs in 1721. It is possible that the eldest son John lived in Congleton, where a John Bostock, junior, a chandler, lived and worked.

Before finishing with this family, let us return to Edward Bostock of Harrop, (born in 1626) brother of Lancelot Bostock. His eldest son Edward also lived in the same place and had a son named Charles in 1648 and a daughter Margaret who died in 1652: his wife died a month after the daughter. He then married a lady called Judith and had a daughter of the same name who died in 1767. Edward left a will in 1697. Edward's other sons, Lancelot and Ralph may have died young as they seem to disappear. However, the fourth son Francis (born in 1635) does occur again. According to the parish registers his children, all born in the 1670s, were Sarah, William, John and Elizabeth. He left a will in 1716. William, son of Francis, died the same year when letters of administration were issued to his sister Elizabeth, wife of Thomas Etchells. Francis seems to have had another son, also named Francis, for following his death letters of administration were issued to his brother John and sister Elizabeth Etchells.

How where the Macclesfield families related to the main line? There are two possible theories. The first relates to the Savage family.

The Savage family were holders of the earl of Chester's manor and forest of Macclesfield, and Sir John Savage, who died in 1495, married Katherine Stanley. Her brother Thomas, the first earl of Derby, was granted the office of

Master Forester of Macclesfield and Steward of the Borough, by king Richard III. From about 1485 these important offices became hereditary. John and Katherine had fifteen children of whom Christopher became, mayor of Macclesfield in 1512. He also held lands within the area of the forest and was often in dispute over his rights with his kinsman the earl of Derby, the Master Forester. In 1510 a survey concerning the extent of land cultivation and enclosure within the forest reveals that Wildboarclough, Harrop, Saltersford and Longside were disputed between these two men. The Stanleys had held interests in these places since 1452.

The grandson of the Savage/Stanley marriage, another John, married Anne, daughter and heiress of Ralph Bostock of Bostock, and their son, John Savage, then became lord of the manor of Bostock. It is possible that the Ralph Bostock who settled in Wildboarclough was a cousin of Ann's and therefore the Savage family. Other members of her kin were provided for by the Savages and became their tenants.

The other alternative is that Ralph is the second son of Ralph of Woodhead (*see below*) and, therefore, descended from the Churton line as the Stanley family seem to have been patrons of that branch and may have provided for a younger son to settle in 'new' lands in Macclesfield Forest. This may be the more favourable suggestion, especially when the names of Lancelot and Edward are found to be common to the Bostocks of Churton, Holt and Macclesfield.

STAPLEFORD

A family of Bostocks settled at Bruen Stapleford, near Tarvin. To whom they are related is not clear, though William Bostock, son of Adam of Bostock, is said by Ormerod to have lived in this township during the mid-fifteenth century.

A John Bostock of Stapleford left a will in 1598 which left his estates to his son Richard and mentions that he bought his lands from Ralph Bostock of Moulton. This son and heir may be the person who appears as a witness to a marriage bond in 1608. Richard also left a will ten years later which mentions his wife, Elizabeth and their children: Richard, Ralph, William, Thomas, Mary, Ann, and Elizabeth.

The next Richard left a will dated 4 September 1651 which states that he was entitled to a messuage and tenement in Broughton, Flintshire. By his wife, Eleanor, he had a son named John who was to inherit the messuage and tenement in Stapleford. Mention is also made of his brother John of Stapleford and brother-in-law Richard Cartwright of Tarvin. The will was proved on 18 January 1655. In 1663 a John Bostock of Fulk Stapleford left a will, as did an Ellen Bostock of Stapleford in 1671. 'Widow' Bostock was assessed on one hearth in the 1663 Hearth Tax returns.

The following marriage licenses exist for Tarvin parish: Richard Bostock and Ellen Ellis, on 5 February 1620 and John Bostock and Ellen Taylor of Tarvin, on 22 September 1629. On 10 August 1709 a marriage bond was issued to Ralph Bostock of Clutton, farmer, for his marriage to Elizabeth Pinnington, at Tarvin: the bondsman was David Bostock of Macclesfield which, as mentioned earlier, suggests a link with East Cheshire.

A branch settled in Broughton, near Chester, which no doubt stemmed from the last mentioned Richard. In 1682 an inventory was made of the goods of John Bostock of Broughton. Eight years later a will of another John of Broughton mentions lands in Flintshire and Cheshire, son Richard and daughter Mary.

TARPORLEY

The history of this family stems from Gilbert Bostock of Bostock, who lived in the thirteenth century and had a son named William who settled in Tarporley, besides another son John who was a chaplain at Chester Cathedral in 1330. William married Margaret, daughter of Thomas Vernon of Lostock, by whom he had John and Margaret (wife of William Weld whose father was sheriff of London in 1352).

The last John's son Thomas was an archer in king Richard II's infamous bodyguard of archers: he also had another son named Hugh whose descendant became the abbot of St Alban's in 1420. Thomas had a son named Ralph who was born in 1384 and married Margaret, daughter of Nicholas Patten of Essex. They had two boys, Roger and John, who became monks at St Albans and died without any children. One of Ralph's two daughters married a Hugh Domelaw of Tarporley (born in 1418) and became heir to her father's estates. Hugh Domelaw had an only son named Richard whose daughter, Isabel, married John Bostock, fourth son of Henry Bostock of Huxley (*see above*). This couple then had two sons and a third who also became a monk at St Albans and two daughters.

John Bostock of Tarporley who appears in the list of Cheshire gentry in 1579 was the great-grandson of the second son of John and Isabel Domelaw. He was born in 1535 and died on 25 March 1597 leaving a son, Ralph, and a daughter Anne. A later John Bostock of Tarporley was assessed on two hearths for the tax returns of 1664. The family also occur in the manorial court rolls for Tarporley.

Robert Chignall Bostock (born 1829) of Kennington, Surrey, produced a small booklet for private circulation in 1903 which traced his family back to Tarporley. The detail of the family in the sixteenth and early seventeenth centuries omits some individuals who occur in the Tarporley parish registers. Particularly an Ellen wife of Ralph Bostock buried on 2 May 1574 and Elizabeth wife of John buried on 16 July 1574 who could have been recorded on his family tree. However there is an Arthur son of Arthur baptised on 25 December 1603 and Margaret daughter of Arthur baptised on 24 January 1607. The younger Arthur went on to have children himself Mary baptised in 1628 and Arthur in 1635. Some family histories have suggested that Arthur's family name was spelled 'Bostik' in the parish registers, but the registers are quite clear as to the spelling 'Bostock'.

TATTENHALL

Tattenhall is a village seven miles south-east from the centre of Chester. A branch of the family settled here during the reign of king Henry V, when Richard Bostock of Tattenhall married Margery, daughter of Thomas Dodd and sister and heiress of Leonard Dodd of Tattenhall. They had the following children: Richard, George, Maud (wife of Peter Egerton), Joan (wife of Thomas Bulkeley of Farndon), and Ellen (wife of a Longdon of Shropshire).

Richard (the second) held lands in both Tattenhall and Barsley. He married the daughter of Ralph Mainwaring of Cheveley, near Huntingdon and had issue: Ralph, Hugh (who died without children), Dorothy (wife of Richard Allen of Tattenhall) and Ann (who married William Dodd in 1595). The eldest son Ralph married Anne, the illegitimate daughter of Sir Richard Egerton of Ridley and had the following children: Richard, Hugh, Robert (later of Cornisham, Bucks), William (who had no children), Anne (wife of Thomas Tattenhall of Peckforton), Mary (wife of Henry Dutton of Wharton) and Katherine (married Thomas Capper of Bunbury in 1608).

Ralph's eldest son, Richard (the third) was born about 1580, and is the first of whom we know a little. He married the daughter and heiress of Thomas Clutton of Carden and Nantwich. This family held lands in Clutton, Chorley, Carden, Edge, Lowcrosse, Tilston, Bickerton, Monks Coppenhall, Church Coppenhall, Wimboldsley, Tiverton, Henhall, Wistastson and Nantwich. Apparently Richard was a well educated man of 'literary tastes' who built Tattenhall Hall. He died in 1630 and was buried at Tattenhall on 30 May. His funeral certificate, dated 6 June, states that he had an illegitimate son named John who was adopted as his heir. The *inquisition post mortem* heard at Middlewich on 18 May 1631 recorded the names of his reputed son John, wife Elizabeth, and a brother Robert then aged 50 years. Witnesses were Ralph Bostock of Moulton and Philip Bostock of Bostock. Richard's wife died in 1664. John, Richard's adopted heir, married Margery daughter of Edward Dutton of Hatton, esquire. He is mentioned in many deeds relating to the family between 1620 and 1639. He and his wife had the following children: Richard, John, Mary, Martha, Rebecca and Elizabeth.

Robert Bostock, Ralph's second son, described himself as 'of Chester', died in 1633 having left a will dated 1 October that year. He had no children but mentions nephews and nieces: Ralph, Mary and Elizabeth, the children of his sister Anne Tattenhall; Richard, Dorothy, Elizabeth, Anne, Katherine and Eleanor, children of his sister Mary Dutton; and Philip, John and Katherine, children of his sister Katherine Capper. His funeral certificate was witnessed by Ralph of Moulton and Philip of Bostock.

This last mentioned John was a lawyer and during the Civil War was clerk to the Council of War for the Commonwealth based in Nantwich. Whilst serving in that office he was found guilty of the following matter:

> On Saturday the xvi of June 1643 John Bostock of Tattenhall, Esqr. Learned in the Lawes, Clerk unto the Councell of Warr at Namptwiche, being taken with the Acte of Adultery with one Alice Chetwode, in the vicarage house in Namptwiche upon the Sabothe daye att tyme of Dyvyne servis was by judgement of the same councell adjudged to stand in the markett place, upon the markett daye, beinge Saturdaye, during most part of the daye, with papers upon his Brest signifyinge his offence, wch was executed according to, with his whore standinge by him.

John married for a second time to Alice, who, in 1670, after John death, married Edward Brassie of Bulkeley. He had a large family some of whom settled in Ireland. By his first wife he had: Ralph (who died in infancy), Richard (born in 1622), Mary, Martha, Rebecca, John, Sarah and Elizabeth. By his second wife he had: Hannah (born 1629), Mariah (who lived in Dublin and died there, a spinster, in 1672), Abigail, Margaret and Samuel. This last named child was declared John's heir by his will. In the Hearh Tax of 1663 John was assessed on a house with eleven hearths and his mother 'widow' Bostock on a house with two hearths. John's home was clearly a substantial mansion. Tattenhall Hall, described as 'a fair house of all brick', was an

Elizabethan brick building with many gables and large bay windows at the south-east end of the village; it is now a farm house.

Tattenhall Hall.
Built by Richard Bostock, c. 1620.

The Bostocks of Bostock held lands in Newton by Tattenhall as well as Tattenhall in the fifteenth century and a branch seems to have settled in Newton. William Bostock of Newton juxta Tattenhall, yeoman, left a will dated 27 May 1659 in which he mentions his wife Margaret (who left a will in 1676), brother John and sister Marie Beckett. He was buried at Tarvin. Margaret's will mentions her sisters Isabell Yates and Mary and brothers Richard Robert and James. An administration of the goods of Richard Bostock of Newton was made in March 1663 which mentions a nephew Peter and a John Joynson.

WOODHEAD

Woodhead is a village situated at the eastern most tip of the old county of Cheshire (now in Greater Manchester). The reason why a branch settled here is not clear, but it is known they were a branch of the Bostocks of Churton (*see above*).

John, third son of John Bostock of Churton was the first to settle here. He had sons Ralph, John, Arthur, Robert and William, of whom the eldest married a local girl, Joan, daughter of John Hollingworth of Hollingworth, esquire (who died in 1599). They had five sons: John, Ralph, Robert, Arthur and

William. A document made by George Hollingworth in March 1623 gives details of Ralph's marriage and children. It also details the fact that Robert Bostock served in Ireland when he was aged twenty, and then as a captain in the Low Countries under Colonel Sir William Stanley, where he died having attained the rank of colonel. It seems that Robert's service career was not altogether distinguished. In 1594 a Captain Bostock, who served with Stanley, is listed as a rebel and fugitive along with sixteen men under his command.[7] Letters in the Salisbury Collection also refer to Captain Bostock and his death in Stanley's service in 1600. In particular there is a letter dated June that year from Edward Cecil to Sir Robert Cecil that gives specific details of the engagement in which he died. It mentions a battle, fought somewhere between the towns of Nuparte and Ostend, between the forces of Archduke Albert, who was seeking to become duke of Flanders, and the English army. The Archduke with 12000 men and twenty companies of horse managed to successfully deal with a vanguard of Germans and Scots sent to hamper his advance on Ostend. As his army advanced upon the English squadrons a long battle ensued during which an English commander Sir Francis de Vere was shot. One of the Archdukes commanders, Sir William Stanley, with his vanguard that consisted mainly of Spanish troops, pushed the English lines back. Eventually, after a long engagement whose outcome was uncertain, the English forces won a victory and managed to capture the Archduke's general, Admerante of Aragon, and the four of the 'Camp Masters' of the army. Sir William Stanley and Colonel Bostock lay dead.[8] Sir William Stanley's son, William was so worried about his father's activities in serving the king of Spain against the United Provinces that he petitioned King James to be allowed to enjoy his father's and grandfather's estates in Cheshire and Staffordshire.[9]

Colonel Robert Bostock features in an interesting document dated 6 March 1623 that proves the family's connection to the Bostocks of Churton and to the Bostocks of Bostock.[10] The statement of descent, requested by his son Captain William was made and signed by his kinsmen George Bostock of Churton and George Bostock of Holt.

> 'Whereas captainne William Bostocke, the sonne of Robert Bostocke, deceased, late colonel in the Low Countries, hath requested us his kinsmen, whose hands are underwritten to signifie how the said Robert, his father, is descended out of our howse. We do hereby signifie, expresse and declare that the sayd Robert Bostocke Was third sonne lawfully begott of Raffe Bostocke of Woodhead in the county of Chester, gent., which Raffe was sonne to John Bostocke, third sonne to

John Bostocke of Churton, in the sayd county of Chester, esq., the which John is lineally and legitimately descended of Bostocke of Bostocke in the county of Chester, as by our pedigree more playnly may appear. In witness whereof we have hereunto put our hand and seals this date 6 March 1623.
Geo. Bostocke of Churton
Geo. Bostocke of Holt. [11]

It seems that Captain William was in need of some evidence of his ancestry to prove his loyalty to the crown with a view to enjoying his patrimony.

A possible relation was William Bostock who was in the service of the duchess of Feria. He was committed to the gatehouse by the Earl of Salisbury for his recusancy. His wife Elizabeth pleaded for his liberty as he was old and subject to illness and needed the attention of his friends; he had then been in custody for two months. The date of the letter is unknown but was probably prior to 23 January 1612 when the Duchess died.

What happened to this family afterwards is not known for sure. There are a few references to men living in Woodhead and neighbouring Broadbottom in the late seventeenth and early eighteenth century but is difficult to be precise about their relationships.

Why then did a branch of the Bostocks of Churton settle in the moorland wastes of east Cheshire? The answer may lie with the Stanley family. Sir William Stanley of Holt, Denbighshire, was granted the lordship of Longendale with lands in Mottram and Woodhead. In 1495, the crown took possession of the lordship on the attainder of Sir William Stanley for high treason and from this time the lordship was continually farmed out to a number of lessees. The Bostocks of Churton were neighbours and tenants of the Stanleys of Holt and one of the Bostock branches actually settled in Holt (*see next chapter*). It was fairly common for the minor gentry to look to the more prosperous to act as patrons and to provide for younger sons in some way. Maybe this is how John Bostock managed to acquire property in East Cheshire: Robert Bostock certainly served Sir William Stanley in the army and may therefore have been a tenant of his.

REFERENCES AND NOTES FOR CHAPTER SEVEN

The sources of information in this chapter have come from a variety of sources. Once again much has been obtained from Ormerod's History of Cheshire. Parish registers and wills lodged at the Cheshire Record Office (Cheshire Archives and Local Studies) have also been referred too.

1. Harl. MS 245 fo. 162.; 139 f.131v; 1424, f.25; 1505, f. 23. The erroneous descents are in Harl. 1500 and 1535 fs. 71, 72.
2. Harl. MS 245, f.162; 1424 f. 25; 1505, f. 23.
3. Harleian MS 245
4. Harl. MS 2151
5. Harl. Ms. 245
6. Much of what follows is from Chaloner, W.H. *Bridget Bostock: the White Witch of Coppenhall* (19848)
7. Calendar of State Papers, Elizabeth, 1591-4, pp546, 558.
8. Salisbury Papers, x, pp 197, 213; xii, p.570.
9. Salisbury Papers, xxiv, p. 209.
10. *Ibid.*
11. Harleian MS 2119, f. 14.

8.   THE BOSTOCKS OF ELSEWHERE IN ENGLAND AND WALES

The family spread over the centuries to many parts of England, Wales and Scotland. Tracing the links between the various branches has been undertaken by Roland Bostock and the results published on his web-site www.bostock.net. The extensive research has produced sixty-seven family trees containing tens of thousands of names. In a book such as this it is impossible to mention all of the branches known about, nor necessary, given the detail available on the Bostock web-site, so in this book I mention just a few branches of particular interest.

HOLT, DENBIGHSHIRE

Holt is a small town on the Welsh side of the River Dee and opposite Farndon. The Bostocks resided at a mansion on the road to Wrexham which is still known as 'Plas Bostock'.

This branch descended form Lancelot Bostock, son of Robert of Churton, by his second wife Dorothy. He was a courtier who was appointed as a Gentleman at Arms in 1560 and through his influence at Court was able to obtain a number of perquisites, such as, in 1572, a grant of fines and penalties for contravention of the laws against pluralities. He was returned as the Member of Parliament for Tamworth in 1572 probably through the efforts of his friend the earl of Leicester. In Parliament, he is recorded as sitting on a legal committee in March 1576. Two years earlier he had been made High Sheriff of the county of Flint and fourteen years later was appointed Constable of Holt Castle.[1] In 1588, he occurs as plaintiff in an enquiry concerning the castle and the right of a person to lodge in the outer gate-house. As early as 1574 and in the *Visitation of Cheshire*, 1580, he is styled 'pensioner' which means he a member of the Queen's Band of Gentlemen Pensioners instituted by King Henry VIII, which is today known as 'Her Majesty's Honourable Corps of Gentlemen at Arms'. At this time the term 'pensioner' as nothing to do with age but simply means being in receipt of a regular payment from the crown.

Lancelot Bostock of Holt, was one of a number of men from Lancashire and Cheshire known as the 'Undertakers of the Province of Munster' and received about 4000 acres in Limerick and for a time he lived in the province, though he was home by the early 1600s.[2] The confiscation of estates in Ireland by the crown had opened up the possibility of a profitable exploitation of land there and suited the government by establishing enclaves of English civilization in the midst of the Irish. It was also intended to provide a ready-made and relatively inexpensive garrison to protect Munster and south-west England against a possible invasion by Spain. Confiscated lands were divided into twenty seigneuries or estates, each containing 12,000 acres of arable land as well as adjoining bog, mountain and waste. These estates were then split into smaller units of 4,000 or 8,000 acres and given to men who undertook to plant on them ninety-one English tenants and their families, each of whom would get a farm of several hundred acres, and also seventy-one household servants. In addition, it was expected that each undertaker would bring in some craftsman, *e.g.* carpenters, stone-masons, and it seemed likely that the government expected to have about 8000 English people settled in Munster eventually. Each undertaker was expected to remove all Irish people from his estate and to pay an annual rent to the government. He was to keep three horse-soldiers and six foot and each of his tenants was to keep one foot-soldier fully equipped for the defence of the colony.

Lancelot married Jane, one of six daughters and heiresses of Richard Roydon of Holt. As the Roydons were an ancient local family that owned much property it may be due to this marriage that Lancelot became settled here. Lancelot died about 1588 and his will was proved on 23 March 1603. The antiquary Laurence Bostock visited his cousin 'Mrs Lancelot Bostocke' at Gresford Vicarage where she was apparently living in mid-November 1581: Lancelot was presumably in Ireland at the time as Laurence doesn't mention him.[3]

George Bostock of Holt married Dorothy, daughter of Hugh Calveley of the Lea. He first appears in 1594 when he was pardoned for the murder of John Roydon, which supposes an interesting story that is now lost: was John a kinsman, was he aggrieved at the Bostock's inheritance in Holt, was the murder a result of a family feud? Whatever, in 1620 George as elected as mayor of Holt. George was buried at Holt on 24 December 1627. His will, proved in 1628, mentions his 'noble and good friend Sir Robert Chumley, baronett' and his brother-in-law Henry Lea. His funeral certificate states that his son and heir George was aged 21 years 'or thereabouts'.

George, the second, seems to have had an active life. During the Civil War George served as a captain in Sir John Owen's regiment of foot and he raised levies in the Holt area for the Royalist armies. He eventually rose to the rank of Lieutenant Colonel in the same regiment. He served as a justice of the peace for the county of Flint and as such signed his name a G.E. Bostocke; the 'E' standing for Edward by which name he was also known. In 1636, he was High Sheriff of Denbigh. He married twice: first to Jane, daughter and heiress of David ap Edward of Dimren; secondly to Katherine, daughter of Hugh Jones of Wrexham. Unfortunately he had no children by either lady.

On 14 August 1663, whilst George was sitting at Llanrush Quarter Sessions, and in the process of binding over a number of people from Wrexham to be of good behaviour, he collapsed and died. We are informed by a man who witnessed the event, that he died from a surfeit of drink! As George had no children, his will, dated 1663, names his heir as Lancelot Williams who was a son to Thomas Williams and George's sister Mary. The will states that Lancelot was to take the name of Bostock and to use the family's coat of arms. George's other sister married Thomas Yale of Plas Yale.

WHIXHALL, SHROPSHIRE

A branch of the Bostocks of Moulton settled at Whixhall, Shropshire. This village is only seven miles west of Moreton Say where there is an effigy to John Bostock of Hassall (_see Chapter 7_).

Robert Bostock of Moulton married Anne, daughter and heiress of Thomas Soulton of Whixhall and Oswestry: they settled in Whixhall and built Bostock Hall there. Thomas Bostock, born about 1520 married Maud Hugenson of Wem and had three children: Robert, Andrew and Ann. He then married Katherine, daughter of Hugh Bryne of Ashton and had George, John, Thomas, Elizabeth, Margerey and Joan. George, Thomas' third son married Margerey, daughter of Roger Shawbury at Shawbury on 3 May 1585. He was followed by George who on 19 July 1629 had a son Richard baptised at the parish church of Upton Magna. This Richard was buried at Prees in 1703. The family line continued to a Nathaniel Bostock, born in 1655, who became a renowned

"Doctor of Physic" and it is assumed that the family sold up to move to a more populated area for him to continue his practice since there is no record of the family after 1717.

The family are mentioned in the _Visitation of Shropshire, 1664_, when Richard Bostock was granted a silver canton on his coat of arms 'for the taking away of all other differences'.

MORETON SAY, SHROPSHIRE

The family that settled here descended from the Bostocks of Hassall, Cheshire. Humphrey Bostock married Eleanor the sole heir of Robert Say of Moreton Say, Shropshire, and thus inherited property here. (*See Chapter 7*) His son, also named Humphrey, who lived during the mid fifteenth century, married his cousin Eleanor, daughter of Sir Adam Bostock, lord of Bostock. Next came Hugh who married Anne daughter of Thomas Poyner of Beslow, Shropshire, and by her had at least two sons, Edward and Edmund (who had an illegitimate son named Richard), and one daughter, Eleanor who married a Mr Farrington of Halton Lodge and then Randoll Smith of Warmingham whose previous wife had been Jane Bostock of Norcroft.

Edward married Anne daughter of John Tittenley of Audlem, Cheshire, and they had at least four sons, Hugh, John, Anthony and Peter, and a daughter named Alice wife of John Butler of Wanswell, Gloucestershire. According to the pedigrees of the Bostocks of Middlewich Edward had a daughter named Tomasin who married William Bostock of Down Hatherley, Gloucester. (*See Chapter 6*) Of the sons the pedigree notes that, John had no children, Anthony married a lady called Isabell, and Peter was slain in Zeeland (Netherlands), near the city of Middlesburg. Hugh married Margaret, daughter of Thomas Lee of Langley, by whom he had: Mary, Jane, Margerey, Anne, Elizabeth, Martha, Margaret, Sarah and John, though John is not mentioned in the pedigree in the Harleian document. Hugh died in 1581 and his *inquisition post-mortem* records that he was seized of lands in Hassall, valued at £3 6s 8d, and lands in Thirlewood, Wheelock. His son was John who was then only four years old.

Hugh's second daughter Jane is celebrated as the lady who in 1598, produced the earliest surviving British example of a type of embroidery work known as a sampler. It was made to commemorate the birth of her cousin, Alice Lee, two years previously. The piece of work is now in the Victoria and Albert Museum in London.

John Bostock died on 21 December 1611 at the age of 34, having married Jane, daughter of Sir Thomas Vernon of Haslington, near Crewe, Cheshire. After his death she became the second wife of Richard Grosvenor, 'late of Eaton', Cheshire. After Jane's death the Bostock estate was divided amongst the families of Richard Grosvenor's sisters. The *Visitation of Shropshire 1623*, published by the Hareian Society gives the arms of the family as consisting of the basic Bostock arms with a martlet for difference quartering '*Or, a lion rampant Sable*' and a crest of a martlet. In the north-east corner of the parish church at Moreton Say there is a particularly fine arched alabaster monument erected in 1625 by Jane to the memory of her former husbands. Three effigies lie on the tomb chest and these represent John, his wife Jane and her second husband Richard Grosvenor who died in 1619: John is in the forward position, Grosvenor is at the rear and slightly elevated to show his superior status and Jane is between them. The whole monument is decorated with the heraldry of Bostock, Vernon and Grosvenor. There is some damage to the monument, for example, the hands of the effigies have gone and, unfortunately, the crests that once surmounted the three helmets at the top have disappeared. *(See Chapter 9)*

The Bostock Tomb at Moreton Say, Shropshire. John Bostock lies at the front.

WHEATHAMPSTEAD, HERTFORDSHIRE

This branch stems from the Tarporley branch. Hugh, son of John Bostock of Tarporley, left Cheshire and settled at his wife's home. He married Margaret, daughter and heiress of Thomas Heyworth of Macerey End, Wheathampstead, near St Albans, Hertfordshire. She had two bothers: John, prior of a religious cell at Tynemouth and William, who between 1401 and 1420, was abbot of St Albans and then bishop of Lichfield from 1420 until his death in 1457.

Hugh and Margaret had a son named John born in 1383. He was educated at St Alban's abbey school before going up to Oxford. He followed his maternal uncles into the church and became prior of Gloucester Hall, Oxford before, in 1420, becoming abbot of St Albans, a position he then held for thirty-two years. John was perhaps the most well known abbot due to his writings on the Wars of the Roses and his accurate account of the second battle of St Albans. In 1423, Wheathamstead attended the Council of Siena, Italy, established to consider church reform. He greatly improved the buildings at St Albans, which suffered somewhat years owing to the Wars of the Roses, the first open conflict of which was the First Battle of St Albans (1455): he also did some building at Gloucester. Much of his time was occupied with lawsuits, several of which he carried on to defend the property and enforce the rights of the abbey. In 1434, John was appointed as arbitrator by John Kingsley and others, including Adam and Hugh Bostock of Bostock and Hugh Bostock of Hassall, to resolve a complicated family dispute. Six years later John withdrew from the abbey due to sickness and dwelt at the family home which he enlarged and improved, but in 1451 he was called out of retirement to resume his role as abbot which then continued until his death. When King Henry VI was injured at the Second Battle of St. Albans in 1461, John had him taken into the Abbey's infirmary for treatment. Having taken a vow pf poverty Abbot John placed his estates into the hands of trustees who at his death, on 20 January 1465, granted his inheritance to John's nephew, John Willey, alias Hayworth. Ormerod says of him 'a chronicler himself of some celebrity, the patron of Lydgate, and a friend of the good duke of Gloucester, distinguished by his honourable epithet of the Wykeham of his day, from his liberality and taste in the restoration of the buildings of his abbey'.

Amongst the monuments of the north transept of Wheathamstead church, on the floor, there is a brass with the representation of a man and his wife – Hugh Bostock and Margaret – below which there are indentations for three sons and three daughters. In each corner there is a shield but only one of these is clear and shows the three bats of the Heyworth coat of arms.

ABINGDON, BERKSHIRE

This branch begins by living in Mobberley, Cheshire and ends up at Abingdon, a small town on the banks of the River Thames in Berkshire.

Nicholas Bostock of Mobberley was the third son of Adam Bostock, lord of Bostock, and would have been born in the mid-fifteenth century. It is alleged that he married Katherine, daughter and heiress of Sir William Mobberley of Mobberley. The couple had three sons: George (who had two daughters), Thomas (whose descendants lived at Tandridge, Surrey), and Hugh whose family now follows.

Hugh lived at Edgerley, a village on Churton Heath. He married Joan, daughter and co-heir to John del Heath, and had three children: George (of Childs Arcall, Salop), John (master of the Holy Cross, Abingdon, 1520), and William (alias Richard who resided at Wem, Salop).

George married Joan, daughter of the Horne family of Childs Arcall and by her had sons Ralph, born circa 1500, and William who died without children. Ralph married Maud Gosling of Longworth and they and their young family moved to Abingdon. Ralph was a university graduate and obtained a Masters degree from Oxford in 1518. When he died in 1556 he left two sons: Anthony and Richard.

Anthony Bostock had a university education and obtained his Bachelor of Arts degree at Oxford in 1514. He became a governor of Christ's Hospital, Abingdon, between 1582 and 1585. This hospital was a charitable institution which was established in 1553 following the dissolution of the Benedictine Abbey in Abingdon to carry out the works previously conducted by the chantry guilds and the Fraternity of the Holy Cross of St Helen's church. The hospital was administered by twelve governors, one of whom was elected as 'Master' and this body wielded much power and influence in the borough of Abingdon. Anthony married twice. First, he married Margery Freare of Weedon by whom he had a daughter. Second, he married Elizabeth Smith of Perchley, Northamptonshire by whom he had two sons – Thomas and William. Thomas was aged 15 when he matriculated at Oxford University in 1581; he went on to receive his BA in 1593 and MA in 1596. Anthony died in 1588 and both his sons seem to have died without any children.

Anthony's brother Richard also had two marriages: first he married Anne Steele of Susses and then Anne Browne of Abingdon. This family continued on for a further three generations in the town and of them we shall deal shortly.

Returning to William Bostock of Wem, he married a Margerey Higginson and had three sons one of whom was Humphrey who also moved to Abingdon and became a wool draper. In 1553 he became a governor of the hospital and remained so for twenty-six years. In 1558 he was elected as mayor of the borough of Abingdon. By his wife Barbara Walker he had a son named Lionel.

Lionel Bostock was born in 1583 and, like his father, he was a wool draper and conducted his business in a house in the town centre called 'the Bell'. About the year 1580 Lionel took a lease on an estate in Abingdon called 'Fitzharris' and there he retired from dealing in wool and lived instead from the profits of land. He, 'by his own industry grew to the greatest estate for wealth an riches of any tradesman in his time'. In 1570 he was elected mayor of the borough and this was repeated in 1577, 1586 and 1594: at his installation in 1577 the earl of Sussex, then Lord Chamberlain, was present. In 1575 Lionel became a governor of Christ's Hospital and was twice elected as the master; he remained a governor until his death in 1600.

On the occasion of his second election as master an argument ensued over his eligibility arising from a feud with the Tesdale family who had been the previous tenants at Firtzharris. Lionel appealed to the Lord Chancellor, who happened to be a Cheshire man Sir Thomas Egerton, who then directed the vice-chancellor of Oxford University to enquire into the matter: the finding was in Lionel's favour.

Lionel Bostock was of a grave and reverend demeanour, a devout church goer and a promoter of numerous lectures and sermons. He died on 5 July 1600 and was buried five days later in St Katherine's chapel in St Helen's church. As he did not leave a will administration was granted by the Prerogative Court of Canterbury to his eldest son, William. Besides this son, Lionel left two other sons, Lionel and Edmund, and a daughter Joan who were the children of his wife Joan, daughter of Thomas Wolley of Henley-on-Thames. Edmund died in 1605 and a plaque was erected to his memory by his brother Lionel.

The tenancy of Fitzharris now passed to William Bostock. He also inherited a considerable estate at Radbourne Cheney, Wiltshire, but sold this in 1606 for £3,100. According to the governors of the hospital Lionel had granted to St Helen's church money for an annual Christmas sermon to be preached by a special preacher chosen by them, and also a weekly bread charity of two shillings. These small gifts failed to appear for nearly a quarter of a century as William refused to pay them. In October 1616, an action for breach of trust was taken against William by the governors. In defence William stated that 'he had not been respected by the inhabitants of Abingdon and had been overcharged in his taxations', but the Commission for Charitable Uses were not convinced an ordered payment of the charities within three years. However William refused to pay up and the governors were forced to take further action eight years later.

Surprisingly, William did become a governor: he served between 1602 and 1624 and was elected master in 1605. He presented the hospital with portraits of himself and his father. The picture of Lionel, commissioned in 1600 when he was 61, shows a sombre old gentleman with a long beard and wearing a fur lined cloak and a black hat and is thought to have been painted by Samson Strong a Dutch artist who lived in Oxford. William's portrait is very different. He is depicted as an Elizabethan gallant wearing galligaskins embroidered with silver thread, and a deep ruff edged with lace. At his elbow on a table lies a beaver hat with a tall plume of ostrich feathers and at his hip can be seen the hilt of a dagger. His portrait is dated 1622 and gives his age as 30. Both pictures show the Bostock coat of arms and crest but in William's portrait the impaled coat of Fitzharris is displayed.

Father and son: Lionel and William Bostock of Abingdon, Berkshire
(Images supplied by Christ's Hospital of Abingdon and used by the author with their permission. They must not be reproduced by any other person)

In December 1592, at Appleton church, William married Edith a daughter of Bessils Fettiplace of Bessilsleigh; she was a grand daughter of Sir John Fettiplace who had been a prominent member of Abingdon society. William was proud of this marriage and of his connections to her family. In 1607 he presented the hospital with a picture of a knight in golden armour which represented Sir Peter Bessils one of his wife's ancestors who, in the fifteenth century, had been a member of parliament for Berkshire and Oxfordshire, a sheriff and the builder of Abingdon bridge. The picture frame was endorsed with the words '*cognationis ergo*' – my blood relative.

Whilst at Fitzharris, William embarked on costly repairs and improvements and had the internal walls clothed in oak panels. In two rooms carved mantelpieces that bore the arms of Bostock and Fettiplace which were still in place in 1929. These building works and other extravagant ways of living caused William to be broke by 1622. He left Abingdon in disgrace and moved to New Windsor where he died. His wife died at Weybridge on 17 June 1643.

Following William's departure the tenancy of Fitzharris was taken by his cousin, Edmund Bostock of Abingdon and Reading (son of Richard Bostock of Abingdon), but not until he agreed to satisfy Lionel's unpaid charities to the satisfaction of the Abingdon corporation. In 1624, Edmund became a governor of the hospital and remained so until his death in 1643; he became master in 1628. He was buried at St Nicholas' church, Abingdon.

Edmund's son William, born in 1610, was a barrister of the Middle Temple. He succeeded his father as a governor but resigned in October 1648 and left Abingdon. His name and pedigree were entered into the *Visitation of Berkshire*, 1665, with the following entry 'Entered gratis upon certification of his losses for the King and present poverty' – the designation 'gent' had been crossed through. It seems that he suffered by adhering to the royalist side in the Civil War, as did his brother Thomas who was slain at Wallingford.

Another William Bostock, son of Thomas and nephew of the last tenant of Fitzharris, settled at Lacey's Court, Abingdon in 1660, and was governor between 1668 and 1677 when he resigned and left the area.

TANDRIDGE, SURREY

Richard Bostock of Tandridge, esquire, was son of Roger and Felice Bostock, and was probably born in Mobberley, Cheshire, around 1530. Richard was educated at St John's College, Cambridge where he read philosophy, mathematics and medicine, and matriculated as a pensioner of St. John's College, Cambridge, at Easter 1545. He went on to study law at the Inner Temple, London. He married twice: Katherine Field and then in 1605 a lady named Jane: he left three daughters Katherine (Fuller), Margaret (Blount) and Jone (Knight): he died in 1612.

He was appointed Escheator of Surrey in 1566, a Justice of the Peace in 1579 and was sheriff of the county in 1585-6. He also served as Member of Parliament for the Borough of Bletchingly on four occasions between 1571 and 1589. He also had to fulfill the wide range of administrative functions that were expected of men of his rank. Records show him attending the assizes in 1579, signing a letter to the Privy Council in February 1579/80, and being appointed a Commissioner for the Muster in 1580.

In 1555, he acquired two estates known as Tandridge Court and Tandridge Priory. He also owned the manors of Oxted, Gaston, and a few other manors in Surrey, and was clearly a wealthy man. In 1600 his estate in Tandridge was assessed on 256 acres. His will, made 17 April 1605 and proved the following 4 April, shows that he possessed a large number of works on divinity, including *The Book of Martyrs.* His interest in alchemy and medicine culminated in with writing and publishing a book entitled *The Difference Betwene the Auncient Phisicke and the Latter Phisicke* in 1585.[4]

In 1590, Richard Bostock was involved in a lengthy dispute with one Foster following his part in the trial and hanging of two of Foster's servants for highway robbery.

ELSEWHERE

Branches also settled in the Americas, Australia, New Zealand and other parts of the world. No matter where they settled the family name of Bostock stems back to one place Cheshire.

The way in which the name spread throughout England and eventually to other parts of the world, is indicated in the illustration in the Introduction.

REFERENCES AND NOTES FOR CHAPTER EIGHT

The sources of information in this chapter have come from a variety of sources. The main source for the Bostocks of Abingdon is A.E. Preston's, *St Nicholas' Abingdon and other Papers* (1929)

1. *Calendar of State Papers Domestic: Elizabeth, 1598-1601*, vol. 269, p. 140
2. *Calendar of State Papers, Ireland, 1588-1592*, pp. 128-141. See also P.W. Hasler, (ed.), *The History of Parliament: the House of Commons 1558-1603*, (1981): http://www.historyofparliamentonline.org/volume/1558-1603/member/bostock-lancelot-1533-c88
3. Hareian MSs. 2113.
4. *The History of Parliament: the House of Commons 1558-1603*, (1981): http://www.historyofparliamentonline.org/volume/1558-1603/member/bostock-richard-1530-16056.

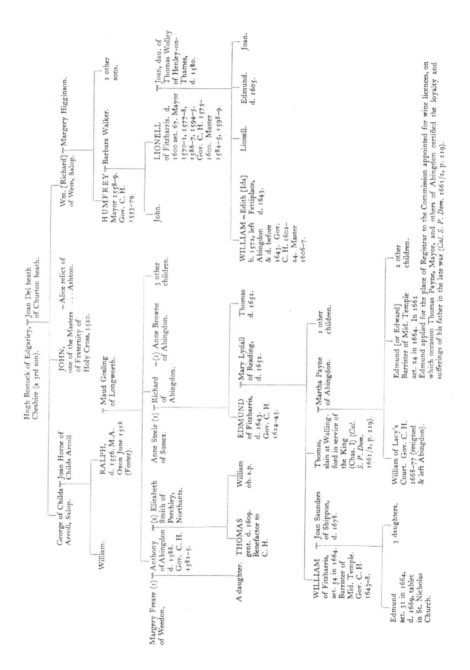

The Pedigree of the Bostocks of Abingdon
(From Preston's St Nicholas' Abingdon and other Papers

9. BOSTOCK HERALDRY

THE BASIC COAT OF ARMS

The coat of arms of the ancient Bostock family is described in heraldic language as '*Sable, a fess humetty* (or '*couped*') *argent*', which means a black shield with a broad horizontal band of silver that is cut-off prior to reaching the edges of the shield. These arms were probably used as early as the thirteenth century by Gilbert de Bostock, though their origins are lost in the mists of time.

The basic coat of arms is similar to those of neighbouring families as regards symbols or tinctures. The Vernons, the original superior lords of the Bostock family, originally bore a gold shield with a blue horizontal bar; the Breretons had a silver shield with two narrow black bars and for a crest had a black bear's head with a red muzzle; the Bulkeleys of Eaton had a black and white shield bearing a chevron between three bull's heads; the Bretts of Davenham had a similar black and white shield with a chevron and three trefoils.

Coats of arms with slight differences were adapted by junior lines of the family and a number of these were illustrated in 1630 by William Smith of Oldhaugh, Warmingham, a Pursuivant of Arms at the College of Arms for a book of arms he compiled for Peter Venables, baron of Kinderton.

**The basic arms of the
Bostocks of Bostock**

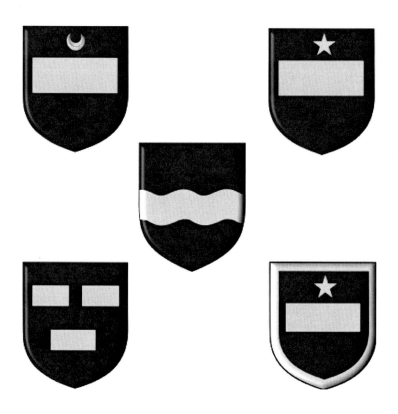

Various differences: from the top, left to right - Churton, Moulton, St. Albans, Middlewich and Belgrave as recorded by Wiliam Smith, 1630

CRESTS

The original crest was '*upon the stock of a tree, erect and eradicated, Or, a bear's head, erect and eradicated, Sable, muzzled, Or*', which means – on a yellow, torn-up tree stump, a black bear's head torn off at the neck and wearing a yellow muzzle. The ancient crest may be a pun on the name, for in old Cheshire dialect the name was pronounced similar to - 'Bear's stock'.

A different crest from the ancient one is given in the *Visitation of 1580: An heraldic antelope statant argent, armed, maned, and tufted, or*. Such a strange beast is best described as having the body of a lion with a downward pointing horn on its nose, serrated horns on its head and the legs of a deer. This monster was used as a badge by King Henry IV and Henry VI to be worn by retainers and adherents, but the *Visitation of Berkshire* says that Adam was actually visited at his home by King Henry IV and granted the antelope crest which the family then used.[1]

The ancient crest and the later heraldic antelope crest

QUARTERED COATS OF ARMS

Over many generations coats of arms can become somewhat complicated with many divisions of the shield known as 'quarterings' being added following marriages to heiresses to form an 'achievement of arms'. When a gentleman married an heiress his son and descendants would 'quarter' the arms of that wife's family together with their quarterings, or a selection of them.

The *Visitation of Cheshire, 1580*, gives a full achievement of arms of the Bostocks of Bostock as borne by the descendants of William Bostock of Bostock, brother of Ralph Bostock, lord of the manor of Bostock.

> Quarterly of fifteen: 1. *Sable, a fess humetty argent.* 2. *Or, a bend azure.* [VERNON] 3. *Quarterly, or and gules, a bend sable.* [MALBANK] 4. *Azure, three garbs or.* [RANDOLPH BLUNDEVILLE] 5. *Azure, a wolf's head erased argent.* [HUGH LUPUS] 6. *Azure, six garbs or.*[HUGH KEVELIOK] 7. *Argent, an orle within eight martlets in orle sable.* [WINNINGTON] 8. *Vert, a cross engrailed ermine.* [WETTENHALL alias KINGSLEY] 9. *Vert, a bend ermine.* [WETTENHALL] 10. *Argent, a fess between three cross-crosslets fitchée sable.* [LAWTON] 11. *Gules, three pheons argent.* [MALPAS] 12. *Argent, a cross flory azure* [MALPAS] 13. *Gules, two lions passant guardant or, a label of five points azure.* [STRANGE] 14. *Azure, two bars argent.* [VENABLES] 15. *Or, on a fess azure three garbs of the field.* [VERNON]

The shield of fifteen quarterings occur from marriages to six heiresses. The second and third quarters represent the alleged marriage of Ralph Bostock to Margaret Vernon, heiress of her father Warin, baron of Shipbrook, and of her

The quarterings of Bostock of Bostock, 1580

mother an heiress of the barony of Wich Malbank. The next group of quarterings come from the alleged marriage between Warin Bostock and Havise, sister and heir of Randolph Blundeville, sixth earl of Chester, and daughter and heir of Hugh Kevelioc, the fifth earl and descendant of Hugh Lupus the first Norman earl of Chester. Havise was by a previous marriage countess of Lincoln and it is possible that the third quarter is not Malbank, but Lincoln, as these coats are similar. The seventh quarter represents the alleged marriage of William Bostock to an heiress of the Winnington family. Numbers eight and nine represent the marriage of Adam Bostock and Margerey Wettenhall, alias Kingsley. The next three quarters come from Isabel, daughter and sole heir of William Lawton of Wyglond and his wife Margaret Wyglond, alias Egerton, an heiress and descendant of the barony of Malpas. The thirteenth coat is something of a problem. It represents the family of Strange with whom there is no known marriage, and they seem to have no part in the genealogy of the Lawtons or the barony of Malpas – strange! The last two coats of arms represent Adam Bostock's marriage to Elizabeth, daughter and heiress of Sir Hugh Venables, baron of Kinderton, who was a descendant of an earlier Venables/Vernon alliance.

The above achievement of arms is unique in the county in that it shows the arms of the earls of Chester along with four of the ancient baronies. Two other families display the arms of the earldom - Mainwaring and Brereton - but even they do not show any of the ancient baronies.

The achievement of arms ascribed to Charles Bostock of London in the *Visitation of London, 1633*, gives the same fifteen quarters described above, for he was a member of that family, with the addition of these five:

16. *Quarterly, argent and gules, in the second and third , a fret or.*
[DUTTON] 17. *Argent, on a bend gules, three escarbuncles*

or. [THORNTON] 18. *Or, a saltire sable.* [HELSBY] 19. *Azure, a chevron between three garbs or.* [HATTON] 20. *Per chevron, sable and argent, three elephants' heads countercharged.* [SAUNDERS] [2]

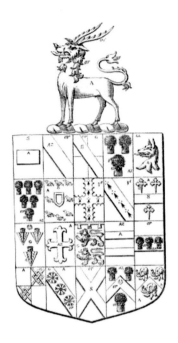

Bostock of London, 1633
From The Visitations of London, vol. i, The Harleian
Society (1880)

Quarters sixteen to nineteen are the arms of the family of Dutton of Dutton. Why did the heralds allow Charles Bostock to include these? Ralph Bostock, lord of Bostock, married Elizabeth, co-heir of Sir Thomas Dutton in 1458, but their only known children were Anne, who married John Savage and William who died without issue. As Charles is a descendant of Ralph's brother William he should not quarter these arms. Was it a matter of ostentation in an age of heraldic importance? Did he allege that his ancestor had been named heir to Ralph? The answer is probably based on a mistake made by the herald William Smith when he drew family tree and wrongly placed Charles' great-grandfather William as son of Ralph and not a brother of Ralph.[3] Interestingly the antelope of the crest is shown *statant* and not *passant.*

The Bostocks of Moulton also have an achievement of arms recorded in *The Visitation of Cheshire, 1580.*

Quarterly: 1. *Sable, a fess humetty argent, a mullet for difference*. 2. *Or, a bend azure*. [VERNON] 3. *Quarterly, or and gules, a bend sable.*[MALBANK] 4. *Azure, three garbs or.* [RANDOLPH BLUNDEVILLE] 5. *Argent, three piles, one issuing from the chief, between two in base sable.* [HULSE] 6. *Ermine, three lions' gambs erased gules, a crescent for difference.* [PICKMERE?]

**The quarterings of Bostock
of Moulton, 1580**

The Bostock shield and the antelope crest are differenced with a mullet which indicates that the branch descend from a third son of the main line. The next three quarterings allude to the marriages of the main family as discussed above. Robert Bostock of Moulton married an heiress of the Hulse family who inherited property from the Pickmere family hence the last two quarters. Why are there no quarterings giving reference to the Moulton family? The arms of that family were: *Gules, between three mullets argent, a chevron of the first, fretty sable*. Other branches who descend from the Bostocks of Moulton do include such a quarter and interestingly the Cotgreave family included it, along with Bostock, due to the fact that one of their sons married an heiress ofWilliam Bostock of Huntingdon. Interestingly, the achievement does not include a quartering for Robert's marriage to an heiress of the Salt family.

The achievement of the Bostocks of Churton in the *Visitation* are:

Quarterly: 1. *Sable, a fesse humetty argent, a crescent for difference*; 2. *Or, a bend azure* [VERNON]; 3. *Quarterly, or and gules, a bendlet sable [MALBANK]*; 4. *Azure, three garbs or* [RANDOLPH BLUNDEVILLE]; 5. *Gules, a lion rampant within a bordure indented or* [DEE]; 6. *Vert, a bend ermine* [WETTENHALL]; 7. *Argent, a scythe erect, Sable* [SNELSTON]; 8. *Azure, three fishes, two in chief and one in*

138

base, their heads meeting in the fesse point argent [SHOCKLACH];
Over all an escutcheon of pretence, *Per pale, gules and azure, a wolf salient or, vulned in the shoulder proper.* [HANKY]

The crescent on the Bostock shield, and also on the crest, denote that the branch stems from a second son of the main line. Quarters two, three and four now need no explanation. Quarter number five alludes to the marriage of David Bostock (son of Adam Bostock) to a daughter of the Dee family, but why the Wettenhall arms appear next is a mystery, unless the Dee family included them. Quarters seven and eight come from Robert II's marriage to Alice, heiress of her father Robert Snelston and her mother a daughter of the Shocklach family. Over all there are the arms of the Hanky family as George Bostock married Ann, the heir presumptive to John Hanky of Churton: their issue would place the Hanky arms as the ninth quarter in the usual fashion if John Hanky died without a son – which he did. The basic shield of arms of the Bostocks of Churton (i.e. Bostock of Bostock with a crescent) and the arms of Bostock of Barton (the same within a silver border) once appeared in a window of Farndon church. At one time, on a pulpit cloth in the same church there were also the arms of Bostock of Churton and Hanky displayed together.

Bostock of Churton, 1580

The funeral certificate of George Bostock of Holt records that family's achievement of arms in 1627.[4]

> Quarterly: 1. *Sable, a fesse humetty argent, a crescent for difference. 2. Or, a bend azure.* [VERNON] 3. *Quarterly, or and gules, a bendlet sable.* [MALBANK] 4. *Azure, three garbs or* [RANDOLPH BLUNDEVILLE] 5. *Gules, between three mullets argent, a chevron of the second fretty*

Sable [MOULTON] 6. *Gules, two lions passant guardant or, a label of five points azure.* [STRANGE?] 7. *Argent, a griffin segreant, per fess gules and azure* [HARGREAVE] 8. *Vert, a bend ermine* [WETTENHALL] 9. *Azure, three eagles displayed or* [ALPRAM] 10. *Argent, a scythe erect sable* [SNELSTON] 11. *Azure, three fishes, two in chief and one in base, their heads meeting in the fesse point, argent* [SHOCKLACH] 12. *Vert, a cross engrailed ermine.* [WETTENHALL alias KINGSLEY] 13. *Argent, a fess gules, between three leopards' faces sable* [LEA] 14. *Azure, three standing dishes argent* [STANDISH] 15. *Argent, a saltire engrailed, between four hammers sable* [YOWLEY] 16. *Azure, a lion rampant argent* [CREWE].

The quarterings Bostock of Holt, 1627

There are a number of matters which need to be considered with this achievement. Quarter number five is shown as Moulton and yet the main line of the family did not show these arms and neither did the Churton branch, from whom the Holt branch descend – why? The next two quarters may be associated with that of Moulton. The arms of the Dee family which are quartered by the Churton line are omitted. Quarters eight and nine are linked as the Wettenhalls had married with heirs of the Alprams. The reasons behind the last four coats is not known.

The arms of the Tattenhall branch are also taken from a funeral certificate.[5] The achievement is a shield of nine quarters:

1. *Sable, a fesse humetty argent, a mullet for difference*; 2. *Or, a bend azure.* [VERNON]; 3. *Quarterly, or and gules, a bendlet sable.* [MALBANK]; 4. *Azure, three garbs or* [RANDOLPH BLUNDEVILLE]; 5. *Gules, between three mullets argent, a chevron of the first, fretty sable* [MOULTON]; 6. *Gules, two lions passant guardant or, a label of five points azure* [STRANGE]; 7. *Argent, a griffin segreant, per fess gules and azure* [HARGREAVE]; 8. *Vert, a bend ermine* [WETTENHALL]; 9. *Argent, on a fess gules, between two bars, wavy, sable, three crescents or* [DODD].

Unlike the previous achievements the crest in this case is the ancient bear's head on a tree stump, though with a black mullet for difference. These arms are as previously discussed as regards numbers one to eight. The last quarter comes from the marriage of Richard Bostock and Margery Dodd.

The arms of Bostock of Hassal and Moreton Say are shown on the tomb of John Bostock in Moreton Say church. He bore four quarters: 1 and 4. *Sable, a fess humetty argent, a martlet or for difference.* 2 and 3. *Or, a lion rampant sable.* [LEE of LANGLEY.] These arms are shown impaled with those of Vernon to represent the marriage to Jane Vernon of Haslington. The arms of Lee should show the lion as having a red tongue and claws. The arms of Lee come from a marriage to Margaret, daughter and heiress of Thomas Lee of Langley. The large shield of arms on the side of the tomb chest shows the arms of each of the persons buried here impaled together. To the left are the four quarters of John's arms, the central twelve quarters are those of Richard Grosvenor, Jane's second husband and the final four those of Jane's father Sir Thomas Vernon of Haslington.

The heraldry on the Bostock tomb at Moreton Say, Shropshire.

The arms of the family of Whixhall, Shropshire follow those of the Moulton branch as expected being a descended of that line. In the *Visitation of Shropshire, 1664,* they are given as:

> 1. *Sable, a fesse humetty argent, a canton of the second*; 2. *Or, a fess azure.* [VERNON]; 3. *Azure, three garbs or* [RANDOLPH BLUNDEVILLE]; 4. *Gules, between three mullets argent, a chevron of the first, fretty sable* [MOULTON]; 5. *Argent, three piles, one issuing from the chief, between two in base, sable* [HULSE]; 6. *Sable, a fesse humetty argent, a canton of the second.*

The canton was used by this branch as a mark of difference and was allowed by the heralds in 1664. The family also used the ancient crest.

The arms of the Bostocks of Abingdon are displayed on a memorial tablet in the church of St. Nicholas, Abingdon and in the *Visitation of Berkshire.*[6] Essentially they are those of Bostock of Bostock but with an extra quartering.

> Quarterly – 1. *Sable, a fess humetty argent;* 2. *Or, a bend azure* [VERNON]; 3. *Quarterly, or and gules, a bend sable.* [MALBANK]; 4. *Azure, three garbs or* [RANDOLPH BLUNDEVILLE]; 5. *Argent, an orle within eight martlets in orle, sable* [WINNINGTON]; 6. *Vert, a cross engrailed ermine* [WETTENHALL alias KINGSLEY]; 7. *Vert, a bend ermine.* [WETTENHALL] 8. *Argent, a fess between three cross-crosslets fitchée sable* [LAWTON]; 9. *Gules, three pheons*

argent. [MALPAS]; 10. *Argent, a cross flory azure.* [MALPAS]; 11. *Gules, two lions passant guardant or, a label of five points azure* [STRANGE]; 12. *Argent, two chevronels gules, on a canton of the second, a cross-crosslet fitchy or* [MOBBERLEY].

The last quarter comes from Nicholas Bostock's marriage to Katherine, heiress of Sir William Mobberley. The family used the heraldic antelope for a crest but with the addition of a red collar around its neck. By the time of the *Visitation of Berkshire* they had made a change to the basic Bostock coat in the first quarter to display a helmet as well as the fess. In all, at this time, there are eighteen quarters of which numbers 2- 6 and 8-16 are as the Bostock of Bostock achievement (see above), the seventeenth shows the arms of Mobberley and the last that of the De la Heath family: *Gules, on a bend, cotised, argent, three moorhens sable*, to represent the marriage Nicholas' son to an heiress of that family. For some reason that eludes me the seventh quarter shows *Azure, a lion rampant argent, semi of fleur-de-lys or* for the Holland family.

Interestingly the antelope of the crest is shown *statant* and not *passant* as with Bostock of London.

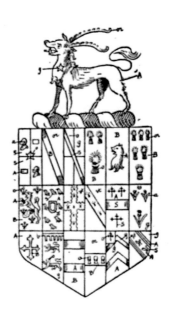

The Quartered Achievement of Arms of the Bostocks of Abingdon,
(from The Four Visitations of Berkshire, 1633, Harleian Society)

In the Bostock residence, Fitzharris, the family arms were once carved on the mantlepiece and on oak panels.[7] In commemorating the marriage of William Bostock and Edith Fettiplace, his and her arms are shown quartered: *Sable, a fess humetty argent;* and *gules, two chevrons argent* . The Bostock arms are also shown with an helmet as a mark of difference. Another carved shield shows: 1 and 4. *Sable, a closed helmet argent.* 2 and 3. *Sable, a fess humetty argent.* In the *Visitation of Berkshire, 1665* we also find: 1. *Sable, a helmet argent and a canton or;* 2 and 3. *Sable, a fess humetty argent;* 4. *Sable, a helmet argent; over all a mullet or.*[7] What prompted this change to the basic coat of arms in the mid-seventeenth century is not clear.

A coat of arms used by a branch of the Bostocks of Abingdon

Some families have had official grants of arms from the College of Arms. Robert Bostock of Otford, Kent, obtained a Grant of Arms in 1733. The description given in a volume of *Miscellanea Genealogica and Heraldica* is: *Argent, a fess humetty azure, on a canton gules a maiden's head couped at the breast, crined or.*[8] The crest is given as *a crescent argent, therein issuant a bear's head, pean, erased gules, muzzled or.* This family descended from a Samuel Bostock who 'came out of the county of Cheshire about 1630 and settled at Chevening, Kent': the arms were granted to his grandson Robert in 1733.

The family who eventually resided at Sittingbourne in Kent had for their arms the basic coat of arms charged with a golden eagle. They also had an adaption of the basic crest changed by having a red muzzle and a branch issuing out of the tree trunk.

Arms and crest of the Bostocks of Otford, Kent

Arms and crest of the Bostocks of Sittingbourne, Kent

REFERENCES AND NOTES FOR CHAPTER NINE

Much of the information in this chapter comes from the various Visitations conducted by the Heralds, notably the *The Visitation of Cheshire, 1580* which was published by The Harleian Society in their volume xviii, (1882).

1. Rylands, W.H., (ed.) *The Four Visitations of Berkshire*, vol. Ii,　vol. lvi,　The Harleian Society (1908), p.76
2. Howard J.J. and Chester, J.l., (eds) *The Visitations of London*, vol. i, The Harleian Society (1880), p. 90
3. Harl. MS 1500
4. Rylands, J.P., (ed.) *Cheshire and Lancashire Funeral Certificates*, The Record Society vol. vi (1882), pp. 27/8.
5. *Ibid*, pp. 28/9
6. Preston, A.E., *St Nicholas' Abingdon and other Papers* (1929); *The Four*

Visitations of Berkshire, p.76
7. Preston, p.464
8. *The Four Visitations of Berkshire*, p.178

OTHER BOOKS BY TONY BOSTOCK

(Available from Amazon in paperback and an E-book formats).

The Chivalry of Cheshire, 1981 (This account of the military activities of the Cheshire Gentry 1346-1400 has been completely revised as an E-book and softback in 2017 and is available from Amazon Kindle).

Owners, Occupiers and Others: Seventeenth Century Northwich, 2004: a study of a Cheshire salt town. Published by Leonie Press. £11.99.

Bostock: A History of a Village and its People (2010).

Winsford: a History of a Cheshire Town and its People (2015). Published by Leonie Press.

Cheshire's Monuments to the Past: I. Mediaeval Effigies (2016).

Cheshire's Monuments to the Past: II. Tudor & Stuart Effigies (2016).

Dog's of War: Sir Hugh Calveley & Sir Robert Knolles (2017).

Of Cheshire Stock: the early history of the Bostock family and the times in which they lived (2017).

Cheshire's Charms: Ancient Villages and Hamlets (2020).

'A Damnable and Sinister Regime': Vale Royal Abbey, 1260-1538 (2020)

The Norman Earls of Chester and their Barons (2022)

Other Publications

(Articles in published journals are shown within quotation marks. The journals are in italics).

'Vale Royal Estate, 1616', *Cheshire History,* vol. 30,1992 and vol. 31, 1993.

'The Heraldic Screens of Middlewich', *Cheshire History,* vol.34, 1994.

'The Origins of Over and Darnhall', *Cheshire History,* vol. 37, 1997.

'The Origins of Over and Darnhall', *Winsford Record,* New Series, 1, 1997.

'The Over Cotton Mill Fire', *Winsford Record,* New Series, 2, 1997.

'Knights Grange - six centuries of history', *Winsford Record,* New Series, 3, 1998.

'The Revolt of the Darnhall Peasants', *Winsford Record,* New Series, 4, 1998.

'17th Century Over', *Winsford Record,* New Series, 5, 1998.

'Darnhall School', *Winsford Record,* New Series, 6, 1998, (editor).

Vale Royal Abbey and the Cistercians 1277-1542, Northwich Heritage Society Publication, 1998.

'Wharton and Winsford in 1841' *Winsford Record,* New Series, 7, 1999.

'A Question of Identity: Cheadle Church's Medieval Effigies', *Cheshire History,* vol. 40, 2000.

'Owners, Occupiers and Others: Seventeenth Century Northwich', *Cheshire History,* vol. 41, 2001.

'A Way Through the Woods', *Cheshire History,* vol. 43, 2003.

'Oulton's Historic Park and Garden', *Cheshire History,* vol. 44, 2004.

'Mapping the Past: Tithes and their value in mapping the past', *Cheshire History,* vol. 47, 2007.

A Hidden Place of Worship: a history of St Chad's church and parish, Over, Winsford. 2007.

St. Chad's Church, Over: a history and guidebook. 2007

'Sir Oliver Starkey, a Knight of Malta', *Cheshire History,* vol. 49, 2009

'An Ancient Mariner and Tudor Hero: Sir George Beeston of Beeston', *Cheshire History*, vol 51, 2011.

'Sir Thomas Holcroft of Vale Royal', *Cheshire History,* vol. 54, 2014.

'Cheshire's Seat of Learning', *Cheshire History,* vol. 55, 2016.

'The Heraldic Screens of Middlewich, Cheshire', *The Coat of Arms*, series 4, vol. 1, 2018.

'"Learned & Langwaged": William Smith (1546-1618), Rouge Dragon Pursuivant of Arms', *Cheshire History*, vol. 57, 2018.

'Five Medieval Cheshire Knights', *Cheshire History*, vol. 58, 2019.

'The Bramall Pew', *The Heraldry Gazette*, December 2019.

'Mary Fitton: The Life and Loves of an Elizabethan Maid of Honour', *Cheshire History*, vol. 61, 2021.